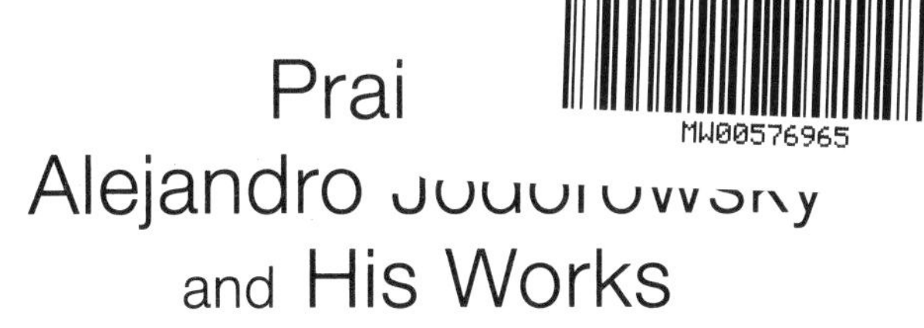

Prai
Alejandro Jodorowsky
and His Works

"Jodorowsky is a brilliant, wise, gentle, and cunning wizard with tremendous depth of imagination and crystalline insight into the human condition."

Daniel Pinchbeck, author of *Breaking Open the Head*

"Alejandro Jodorowsky seamlessly and effortlessly weaves together the worlds of art, the confined social structure, and things we can only touch with an open heart and mind."

Erykah Badu, artist and alchemist

"His films *El Topo* and *The Holy Mountain* were trippy, perverse, and blasphemous."

Wall Street Journal

"The best movie director ever!"

Marilyn Manson, musician, actor, and multimedia artist

"An autobiographical work by an octogenarian, *The Dance of Reality* begs to be read as a culminating work. . . ."

Los Angeles Times

"*The Dance of Reality* [film is] a trippy but big-hearted reimagining of the young Alejandro's unhappy childhood in a Chilean town. . . ."

New York Times Magazine

"Rather than clarifying the meaning of his imagery, [*The Spiritual Journey of Alejandro Jodorowsky*] only inspires readers to enjoy its 'mystery' . . . a worthy read, filled with growing pains and crises that end in artistic triumph and achievement of wisdom and compassion."

SCENE4 MAGAZINE

Manual of Psychomagic

The Practice of Shamanic Psychotherapy

Alejandro Jodorowsky

Translated by Rachael LaValley

Inner Traditions
Rochester, Vermont • Toronto, Canada

Inner Traditions
One Park Street
Rochester, Vermont 05767
www.InnerTraditions.com

Text stock is SFI certified

Originally published in Spanish under the title *Manual de Psicomagia* by Ediciones Siruela
First U.S. edition published in 2015 by Inner Traditions

Library of Congress Cataloging-in-Publication Data
Jodorowsky, Alejandro.
[Manual de psicomagia. English]
Manual of psychomagic : the practice of shamanic psychotherapy / Alejandro Jodorowsky ; translated by Rachael LaValley.
pages cm
Translation of: Manual de psicomagia.
Includes index.
ISBN 978-1-62055-107-3 (paperback) — ISBN 978-1-62055-161-5 (e-book)
1. Magic—Psychological aspects. 2. Medicine, Magic, mystic, and spagiric. 3. Shamanism. I. Title.
BF1623.J6313 2015
131—dc23

2014028429

Printed and bound in the United States by Lake Book Manufacturing, Inc.
The text stock is SFI certified. The Sustainable Forestry Initiative® program promotes sustainable forest management.

10 9 8 7 6 5 4 3 2 1

Text design by Priscilla Baker and layout by Debbie Glogover
This book was typeset in Garamond Premier Pro with Helvetica Neue and Gill Sans MT Pro as display fonts

Contents

Introduction to Psychomagic

Freeing the Shackles of Memory

After having studied and memorized the seventy-eight Arcana of the Tarot of Marseille, I signed a contract with myself: "Once per week, in whatever popular café, I will give free Tarot readings. This I will do until the end of my life." I have been completing this promise for more than thirty years. I turned the Tarot reading into a kind of synthetic psychoanalysis that I call "tarology." Essentially, the goal of tarology is not to guess the future but rather, guided by the Arcana, question the consultant about the past in order to help him or her solve current problems. People of all ages, nationalities, and social, economic, and consciousness levels come to the café where I read their Tarot. There is no lack of those who ask for my advice (the background being a need for permission to do what one dares not do) or for a divination (as positive as possible). I must, therefore, frame each question.

"Am I going to meet a man?"

I cannot tell you if you are going to meet a man, but I can tell you why you haven't met one.

"Should I leave my wife and children for a lover?"

I cannot tell you if you should or should not do this or that thing, but I can tell you the reasons that you have to continue living with your family and the reasons that you have for going with the other. Weighing the advantages and disadvantages of both, you must choose what most suits you.

All predictions and advice are takeover attempts designed by the Tarot reader to convert the consultant into the "magician's" subject. When the consultant no longer considers the unconscious an enemy and loses the fear of being him- or herself, the consultant can uncover the trauma causing the suffering. When this happens, he or she tends to ask for the solution.

"Okay, finally I know I am in love with my mom, which impedes my forming a stable relationship. Now, what do I do?"

"Yearnings to give old men oral sex torment me because, when I was a child, my grandfather put his penis in my mouth. How do I liberate myself from this?"

Having confirmed to myself that sublimating the undesirable urge either through an artistic activity or through acts of social service does not eliminate repressed desires, I invented psychomagic.

Psychoanalysis is a technique that heals through words. The consultant, who is called "the patient," sits back in a chair or on the sofa. The psychoanalyst is, at no time, allowed to touch the patient. To free the patient from his or her painful symptoms, he or she is only asked to recall dreams, take note of slips and accidents, separate from the language of the will, and say, without breaks, whatever comes to mind. After a long time of confusing monologues, the patient sometimes manages to revive a recollection, buried in the depths of his or her memory.

"They changed my nanny."
"My little brother destroyed my dolls."
"They forced me to live with my smelly grandparents."
"I surprised my father making love to a man," and so on.

The psychoanalyst—who helps the patient progress by converting the messages sent by the unconscious into a reasoned discourse—believes that, once the patient discovers the cause of his or her symptoms, the patient can eliminate them. But it does not end like this! When an unconscious urge emerges, we can only be released by fulfilling the urge.

Psychomagic proposes that we act, not just talk. The consultant, following a path contrary to that of psychotherapy, instead of teaching the unconscious to speak a rational language, learns the language of the unconscious, which is composed not only of words but also actions, images, sounds, smells, tastes, or tactile sensations. The unconscious is capable of accepting symbolic or metaphoric fulfillment: a photograph of someone can represent the actual person or a part can represent the whole (such as witches casting a spell with hairs of their potential victim). The unconscious projects, from memory, the person onto another being or object. The creators of psychodrama realized that someone who agrees to play the role of a relative can provoke deep reactions from a consultant, as if the relative were standing there in person.

Punching a cushion produces relief from anger toward an abuser. But to achieve good results, the person who punches the cushion must, in a way, free herself from any morality imposed by the family, society, and culture. If the consultant does this, she can, without fear of punishment, accept her (always amoral) inner urges. For example, if someone wants to eliminate his little sister, because she attracts the mother's attention, and pins a photograph of the little one onto a melon and busts the fruit apart with a hammer, his unconscious assumes the crime is done. This way, the consultant feels liberated.

It is understood in psychomagic that those who populate the internal world (the memory) are not those who populate the exterior world. Traditional magic and witchcraft work with the exterior world, believing in the ability to acquire supernatural powers by way of superstitious rituals in order to influence things, events, and beings. Psychomagic works with the memory. Given the previously cited case, it is not about eliminating the flesh-and-blood little sister (who is now an adult) but about eliciting a change in memory—as much in the image of the hated one when she was young as in the accumulated feelings of helplessness and rage in the one who hates. To change the world it is necessary to begin by changing ourselves. Images retained in the memory are accompanied by perceptions of ourselves at the moment when we had the experiences. When we remember our parents just as they acted during our childhoods, we do so from an infantile point of view. We live accompanied or dominated by a group of egos at different ages—all of them manifestations of the past. The goal of psychomagic is to convert the consultant into his or her own healer and to assure that the consultant is placed within his or her adult ego: the ego that cannot occupy any other place but the present.

I began to propose acts of psychomagic to my Tarot consultants. They were custom tailored, corresponding to each person's character or story. I wrote about some of these experiences in my books *Psychomagic* and *The Dance of Reality,* which had a large impact. The requests for help increased, so much so that I was not able to respond to them all. For those with whom I had time to work, I requested that they, after fulfilling the act, send me a card describing the results. Based on the acts that had a healing effect, I then began to compile psychomagic tips that could be used by a large number of people. This book of "recipes" is the product of endless experimenting.

Note to the reader: To avoid repetitively using "he or she" and "his or her" constructions, gender pronouns are alternated to achieve balance.

ONE

Psychomagic Tips to Heal Your Life

Authenticity, Health, and the Influence of the Family Terrain

For good results it is necessary for the person who wants to practice psychomagic to have an understanding attitude toward himself. Children, in their effort to be loved by their parents, fear being judged guilty of an offense. For a child, who depends vitally on adults, it is terrifying to awaken anger in the adult and to be punished. Children learn to deny or repress what Freud called polymorphous perversity—infantile sexual desires toward any object (loosely speaking). This primary, innate amorality must be accepted when one works to eliminate the effects of trauma. The experimenter must accept his urges—whether incestuous, narcissistic, bisexual, sadomasochistic, cannibalistic, or coprophagic—and fulfill them metaphorically. Beneath every illness is the forbiddance of something we desire to do or an order to do something we do not desire. All recovery requires disobedience to this prohibition or order. And in order to disobey, it is necessary to lose the infantile fear of not being loved or the fear of abandonment. This fear provokes a lack of confidence: the affected does not realize who she actually is and instead tries to be what others expect her to be. If this person persists in this attitude, she transforms her innate beauty into an illness. Health only finds itself in the authentic. There is no beauty without authenticity. To arrive at that which we are, we should eliminate that which we are not. The greatest happiness is to be what one truly is.

A psychomagic act is most effective if the consultant fulfills the following requisites.

1. Metaphorically fulfill the predictions.

Parents register words in the memories of their children that act as predictions later. Accompanied by their parents' orders and prohibitions, the brain of the adult tends to act them out. For example:

> "If you stroke your genitals as a child, when you are older you will be a prostitute."
>
> "If you don't follow in the professional footsteps of your father and grandfather, you will die of hunger."
>
> "If you are not obedient, when you grow up they will put you in jail."

These predictions, at the time of adulthood, turn into agonizing threats. The best way to be free of these predictions, as the reader will see upon reading the recipes, is to fulfill them in a metaphorical way: that is to say, instead of rejecting the threat, surrender to it.

2. Do something you've never done.

The family, in collusion with society and culture, builds innumerable habits in us: We eat one kind of food. We have a limited number of perceptions, ideas, feelings, gestures, and actions. We surround ourselves with the same things. To heal, we must change our point of view toward ourselves. The "I" who endured the illness is younger than I am; it is a mental construction imprisoned in the past. Upon freeing ourselves from the vicious cycle of our habits, we discover a more authentic and, therefore, healthier personality. Carlos Castañeda made a very successful businessman (and Castañeda disciple) dress poorly and sell newspapers on the street in the city. The occultist G. I. Gurdjieff (1877–1949) demanded that a student, who was an inveterate smoker, quit smoking, and until he quit, Gurdjieff forbade any visit from him. The student fought for four years against the habit. When the student managed to overcome his habit, he very proudly presented himself in front of the teacher: "So! I quit smoking!" Gurdjieff responded, "Now, smoke!"

Ancient black magic employed charms made of revolting products, such as fecal matter, parts of human cadavers, and animal poison, considering each impure, and also rare, ingredient of a certain effectiveness. For this reason, psychomagic advice, at times, includes material considered dirty or promiscuous by most.

3. This must be understood: the more difficult it is to fulfill an act, the more benefits will be obtained from it.

To heal or to solve a problem we need an iron will. To not do what we desire to do or to not do what we do not desire to do causes us a deep lack of self-esteem, which causes depression and serious illnesses. The tireless battle to fulfill a goal that seems impossible develops our vital energy. Medieval sorcerers understood this very well when creating formulary that proposed to perform impossible acts, for example, a method to make someone invisible.

> In a cauldron, boil blessed water over white vine firewood. Submerge in it a live black cat, leaving it to cook until the bones fall away from the meat. Extract these bones with a bishop's stole and hang it in front of a sheet of polished silver. Put the blanched cat, bone by bone, into your mouth until the image disappears from the silver mirror.

Another example: to seduce a man.

> In a glass made by hand with clay excavated by a wild boar's snout, mix together the blood of a dog, the blood of a cat, and your menstrual blood. Add a ground pearl to this. Dissolve ten drops of this brew in a glass of wine and give it to your lover to drink.

In the first example, one could think that the spell refers to what must become transparent—which is the individual self of the aspiring sorcerer—rather than think in terms of material invisibility. After the aspiring sorcerer tries so hard to achieve something so cruel and difficult, the individual personality disappears and the essential self appears, which is, essentially, impersonal. In the second example, it is conceivable that if the witch, for the love of a man, did manage to find mud excavated by a wild boar, assassinate a dog and a cat, and sacrifice money by grinding a pearl to dust, achieving this would awaken such a sense of security in her that she would become capable of seducing a blind, deaf mute.

In a similar fashion, miraculous remedies available in faraway places are miracles largely because the patient must make a long and costly voyage to obtain them.

4. Always end an act in a positive way. Adding bad to bad changes nothing.

In the practice of the kosher Hebrew diet, when instruments that were in contact with dairy products come into contact with the flesh of an animal, making them impure, the instruments are buried in the earth for a certain number of days. At the end of this time, the instruments are extracted: the earth has purified them. Inspired by this, I have recommended many times to consultants to bury objects, such as clothes or photographs, to free themselves from past sufferings. But I have always also asked that the consultant plant a tree or floral plant in the place where she buried the "impure" things. If I recommend to a consultant to let out the rage against someone accumulated over many years by tearing up a photograph or kicking a tomb or writing a letter of confrontation, I recommend that he smear the photograph with rose jam, write a love letter on the tomb with honey, or send the person with whom a reparation is needed a bouquet of flowers, a box of candies, or a bottle of liquor. The psychomagic act must be transformative: the suffering giving rise to a friendly end. Hate is love that has failed to be returned.

Reading these tips, the consultant may think them impossible because there will be annoyed witnesses or negative circumstances. I have found that when a consultant begins a psychomagic act, a mysterious relationship is produced between the individual intention and the exterior world. The place the consultant once feared is suddenly overrun by curiosity and, at the moment of action, is empty. What seems impossible to find, a neighbor offers to the consultant.

A professor, complaining of an imbalance, asked me for a psychomagic act. I recommended that he study with a circus artist to learn to balance himself on a wire cable. He said this was not possible because his school and his home were in a small village in the south of France where it would not be possible to find a circus artist. I asked him to stop thinking of the act as something impossible and that he trustingly let reality come to his aid. Some days later, he discovered that the father of one of his students was a circus artist, a retired tight-rope walker. The consultant found his teacher a couple of miles away.

In these tips, sometimes I advise the consultant to change her name. This first "gift" bestowed on the newborn adapts her within the family. The child psyche, much like that of a domestic animal, identifies with the sound that is constantly used to attract her attention. Finally, she incorporates this name into her existence as if it were a vital organ. In the majority of cases, names slide in the familial desire for its ancestors to be reborn: the unconscious can disguise this presence of the dead not only by repeating the whole name. In many families the eldest son takes the same name of his father, his grandfather, or his great-grandfather; the eldest daughter may take a masculinized name, for example Frank to Frances, Mark to Marcy, Bernard to Bernadette. This name, if it comes loaded with a history or, at times, secrets (suicide, venereal disease, the shame of incarceration, prostitution, incest, vice—from, perhaps, a grandfather, an aunt, a cousin), is turned into a vehicle of suffering or behaviors that, little by little, invade the recipient's life.

Some names bring lightness; others are heavy. The former type acts as a benevolent talisman. The latter is detestable. If a daughter receives, from her father, the name of his former lover, the daughter is turned into her father's girlfriend for life. If a mother, who has not resolved the incestuous knot with her father, names her child after the grandfather, then the son—imprisoned in the oedipal trap—will be driven toward becoming the invincible opponent and driven to imitate that favored (and at the same time hated) ancestor. Some people who receive names of sacred concepts (Saint, Pure, Incarnation) may relate to them as orders and suffer from sexual conflicts. Some, baptized as angels (Angel, Raphael, Gabriel, Celeste), may feel themselves disembodied. For men named Pascal, Jesus, Emmanuel, Christian, or Christopher, it is very possible that they will suffer from delusions of perfection and, at the age of thirty-three (the age that Christ was crucified), will have anxiety about death, accidents, economic ruin, and terminal illnesses. At times, given names are products of an unconscious desire to solve painful situations. For example, a man separated from his mother at a young age names his son Jonathan-Mary and fulfills, in this dual name, his desire to unite with her. If a child dies, the next child may be named Renee (from the Latin *renatus,* which means "revived" or "born again"). To annul the shame of the family, if an ancestor was arrested for having committed a robbery, a direct descendant may be given the name Innocence. If a woman with an incestuous fixation marries a man sharing the name of her father, her son may unconsciously suffer from generational confusion by living as a son to his grandfather and looking upon his mother as a sister, which causes immaturity. If, after the elder daughter is born, a son is born and is given a masculinized version of her name (Anita followed by Anthony, Francine followed by Frank), it may reveal that the birth of the baby girl was a disappointment, and the little boy, considered the blueprint for a future man, may live submerged in painful self-contempt, feeling incomplete. A name taken from stars of the cinema or television or from famous writers imposes a goal that demands fame, which can be distressing if one does not have an artistic talent. If parents transform their child's name into a diminutive (Katie, Jimmy, Rosie, Matty), this can fasten the child forever in childhood. The unconscious, by its collective nature, conceals meaning in names that the individual endures without consciously knowing. The names of saints encourage virtues but also transmit martyrdom. A Mary may be besieged by the desire to beget a perfect son. A Joseph may have difficulty satisfying a woman. They cut off Saint Valeria of Milan's head: women who receive this name may tend toward madness. A Mercedes, a name descending from the Latin *merces* (salary, pay), could be tempted by honestly exercised commerce.

Names, to the unconscious, function as mantras (verses taken from the Vedas and used like charms). These words, by their constant repetition, give rise to vibrations that produce certain mysterious effects. The Brahmans believe that each sound in the physical world wakes up a corresponding sound in the invisible realm and incites into action one force or another. According to them, the sound of a word is an efficient magic agent and the principal key to establishing communication with immortal entities. For the person who from birth to death repeats and hears repeated his or her name, this functions as a mantra. But a repeated sound may be beneficial or harmful. In the majority of cases, the name strengthens a restricted individuality. The ego states, "I am like this and no other way," loses fluidity, and stagnates.

The great devotees of magic, like Eliphas Levi, Aleister Crowley, or Henri Corneille-Agrippa, asserted that the human being has two bodies—one physical and the other light (also called the energetic body or soul), which, being sacred, could not have a personal name. The name that it pronounced, united like a leech attached to the physical body, only reveals the illusory individuality of the person. The body of light forms part of the unpronounceable name of God. The purpose of these magicians was to develop or wake up this body of electricity, integrating it into daily consciousness. If one reaches a functional balance between the body of electricity and the physical body, the selfish ego is eliminated. Upon ceasing to be chained to the first name, this awareness opens the door to freedom for the essential being.

The reader may be surprised to notice that this manual is not ordered alphabetically or thematically, presenting the advice in an apparent disorder. This is because I tried to create a book that, apart from responding to queries on specific topics, can be read immediately, from beginning to end, as if it were a novella or treatise. Each time, in my long activity as a tarologist, I analyzed the consultants' problems, even though they were current, I always ended up discovering that the roots of the problem were found in the family terrain. Childhood influences one's entire life: if there is no balance, the "trio" (mother-father-son/daughter) will create in the individual a destiny sown with multiple failures, depressions, and illnesses. This is why the first tips or pieces of advice introduce the reader to the basic aspects of his or her genealogy tree then stroll through a wide range of psychological, sexual, emotional, and material problems and end with a description of a birth massage (a ceremony intended to give information about the balanced family to which every human being has the right to be born).

All illness is accompanied by spiritual suffering. These tips do not, in any way, intend to replace medical treatment; they only propose solutions for the psychological distress that no pill or surgery can calm.

1. SEXUAL DEVALUATION OF THE FEMALE

In this world governed by men, many women grow up confused because capital value is given to the phallus, dismissing the female sex to the point that it has come to be called *raja,* a word meaning, among other things "a crack, an opening, or a rupture of something." In Mexico, it is called *hachazo.* In many women, this undervaluing, which describes their sex as a castrated penis, produces feelings of inferiority.

- To act with confidence in society, it is very effective for the consultant to insert one or several (according to the intensity of the confusion) gold coins into her vagina. These coins, kept in complete secret, will give her the conviction that she carries something much more valuable than what is found in men's trousers.

At times, the root of this vaginal devaluing is due to the men of the consultant's genealogy tree, who, for many generations, discounted the women and regarded menstruation as a defect.

- The consultant, to increase the value of this biological process, must paint on white fabric or cardboard a self-portrait with her menstrual blood. If the consultant has reached menopause, she must get a younger friend to permit her to dip her fingers into her friend's vagina to stain them with blood and complete the self-portrait. The biggest features must be produced with the fingers; for the fine details, a brush is used. The consultant completes the painting by varnishing it, and then frames it in a silver frame: silver is a lunar color, and the moon is an ancient symbol of the cosmic mother, absolute femininity. She hangs it for a time somewhere in the house that is visible to all visitors. Afterward, she sends it as a gift to her father.

If the desire for social affirmation is intense:

- The consultant paints a medallion with her menstrual blood to wear visibly hanging around her neck.

With very good results, I advise any woman who never felt recognized by her parents—because they hoped for a boy not a girl, which caused ever more and more psychological distress and deep pain—to do the following:

- With the menstrual blood, the consultant stains her face and goes out to visit friends and relatives.

  With a woman who felt ashamed to do this, I advised her to paint a heart on her chest with her menstrual blood each month for one year.

2. FEMALE SHYNESS

Many girls, influenced by the strong personalities of their strong masculine parents, grow up with a shyness that makes it difficult for them to speak up for themselves, move freely, and express their feelings. In order to be liberated from this bothersome psychological prison, my advice to the consultant is:

- The consultant should attend a belly dancing class and, in this way, recover her natural feminine movements. Or she could take singing lessons, not to succeed in this art but to make the voice descend down the throat toward the region of the ovaries: as long as the impulse of words does not arise out of the belly, she will act like a child and not like an adult. Also, the consultant could join a shooting club to learn to shoot a pistol, a rifle, and, if possible, a machine gun. This will teach her to express her thoughts and emotions with conviction and strength.

For women who, in childhood, were orphans, were boarded, were raised by grandparents, or were adopted, and therefore separated from their biological parents, and whose lives have been affected by phrases such as "Whosoever doesn't work also doesn't eat" or "You earn bread by the sweat of your brow," which has caused these women to feel a sense of abandonment and to feel that they must fight tooth and nail for a place in the world (meanwhile, they never feel prosperous or happy), I give this advice:

▶ The consultant buys three gold coins and jogs, carrying one of them in her left hand, another in the right hand, and the third in her mouth. At the end of the jog, she wets the three coins with sweat, puts them in a condom, inserts them into the vagina, dresses up, and goes for a stroll in a very busy place.

She will feel better than ever. Each time she is depressed, she repeats this act.

3. SEXUAL DEVALUATION OF THE MALE

In order for a boy to later feel like a virile adult, it is necessary to count on the presence of a father whom the son can incorporate as an archetype. If this father does not fulfill his paternal role (being absent, denying the son, competing with him, or just behaving in an indifferent, weak, or sickly way), the son will grow up to be timid or insecure, requiring enormous efforts to assert himself in society. His unconscious does not know what it is to feel in his body the weight of a strong sex. To repair this, I recommend:

▶ The consultant gathers several $500 bills (if he doesn't have them he can borrow them); the more the better. He rolls them lengthwise (putting them one over the other) to form a tube and ties them like that with an elastic band. Next, he finds two large marbles or, failing that, two Chinese metal balls used for relaxation. The consultant puts on tight underpants and places these three objects in them: the tube symbolizes the phallus, the metal balls the testicles. With this weight between his legs, he fulfills social and romantic commitments while keeping such an act in strictest secrecy. His shyness will vanish.

On another occasion, the consultant can also use edible, non-toxic paint (used for baking) to paint the testicles and the soles of the feet red. This will bestow on him great strength and security in himself.

4. PREMATURE EJACULATION

The man, in a sexual sense, sits between power and powerlessness. The woman sits between satisfaction and dissatisfaction. He aspires to the satisfaction of being powerful. She aspires to the power to achieve satisfaction.

When the feeling of an inability to satisfy a woman is triggered in a man, due mostly to problems experienced during childhood—causing feelings of failure—the best way to solve this difficulty is to entirely surrender to this defeat instead of seeking power and triumph over it.

- The man affected must use a stopwatch to precisely measure the usual duration of coitus. For example, perhaps it takes him six or eight seconds to ejaculate. Once the time is established, the consultant should make a decision to exceed his record and, under strict measurement, ejaculate in half the time: if it is six seconds, then three; if it is eight, then four. This voluntary dive into failure will force the unconscious to fail in an attempt to fail.

A person to whom I gave this practice told me the next day, regretfully, "Fucking my wife and trying to reach an orgasm in half the usual time, I worked for a half hour but couldn't ejaculate."

5. REJECTION OF SPERM

During a meditation workshop, I asked every male participant to concentrate on his penis and, being aware of his feelings, enter through the urethra and go to his testicles. Once there, I asked each man to describe what was contained there. I obtained some surprising responses: "I feel they are full of shit," "disgusting matter," "a poisonous jelly."

Searching for the cause of these unpleasant feelings, I found that the majority of the men who felt this way were born to mothers who had been tricked or abused by men. These mothers had begat children for whom they sacrificed their lives; the women had had multiple abortions or painful deliveries or had been abandoned. To such women, the sperm becomes a hideous danger. The son, upon sensing this maternal regret, grows up detesting his semen.

No archetype is more powerful than that of the mother. Just as her love that awakens us is great, the terror it can inspire is just as great. For the inner child, she is all powerful. However, there is a unique archetype that is more powerful than the mother: it is the Virgin Mary (or her derivatives, such as the different saints). Even if we are not believers, our unconscious bestows magic power to saints.

▶ The consultant should buy a church candle and, taking care to preserve the wick, melt the wax into a container, then masturbate in the presence of a photograph of his mother and ejaculate in the candle container, mixing the melted wax with the vital matter. Once the wax hardens, he takes this candle to a temple, places it at the feet of a statue or painting of the Virgin, lights it, and leaves it there to burn away.

After this act, the consultant's unconscious will accept that his sperm has been cleansed of any maternal hex and is now purified and blessed.

6. INCESTUOUS DESIRES

A conscious adult is capable of distinguishing between the four languages of communication: the intellectual (with its words and ideas), the emotional (with its feelings), the sexual (with its desires), and the physical (with its actions). He or she knows not to mix love for relatives with sexual desire and not to divert attention away from social obligations. Children are different. A child acts as a whole—gestures, thoughts, feelings, and desires are of the same brick—and pays no attention to moral boundaries. A child's impulses are emotional and sexual at the same time. If parents do not understand this, they reject their child's actions and consider them perverse. For example, if the son tries to touch his father's penis or tries to gratify his sex by rubbing against his mother, or if a daughter tells her father that she wants to be his girlfriend and have a child with him, the parents confer guilt on these natural gestures, suppressing the urge. This urge (which in childhood is healthy and necessary), because it is unsatisfied, persists in adulthood, becoming an incestuous obsession. I know of a case with a dear child who, when her father exited the bathroom nude and she looked with fascination at his sex, her mother slapped her hard, causing her problems as an adult to form relationships.

To people punished in this way, no lover can satisfy them. The desire to make love with the mother or father is revealed in dreams or in verbal mishaps. Mixing up the parent's name with the consort's name, they seek older people, preferring partners who are dominant or married with children. Many times they marry people who share their parents' first names, or they always have partners who are inferior to their parents—the mother-in-law cooks better, has better taste, is more elegant; the father-in-law is stronger, more intelligent, more loving.

To get out of this oppressive situation, I recommend that they fight not against the desire for incest but to recognize it and fulfill it metaphorically.

- Without the mother or father knowing, the consultant should borrow the parent's suit and, if possible, underwear that has not yet been washed and make love to his or her lover while dressed in these clothes. At the moment of orgasm (real or faked), the consultant calls out the mother or father's name rather than the lover's name. After coitus, the consultant cleans the clothes and sends them, wrapped as an anonymous gift, to the mother or father, adding to the package a box of chocolates (mother) or a box of cigars (father).

This act can also work if the desire is present between siblings. If the consultant is homosexual, I recommend dressing the lover with the father or mother's clothes. At the moment of orgasm, the consultant should scream out, as loud as possible, the parent's name.

7. MOTHER-DAUGHTER SYMBIOSIS

The mother whose unresolved narcissistic impulse (she, herself, is the object of her desire) has turned into a knot (when punished, a healthy and necessary childish urge becomes a pathological wish later) can turn her daughter into a mere extension of her ego. Seeing the daughter as a mirror, she does not recognize individuality. The mother has taught the daughter to see the world through her eyes. She has made her an accomplice to her sexual intimacies. This daughter has come to wear her hair and makeup like the mother and dress like her. (I know of this case: a painter who thought her daughter's greatest amusement was watching and listening to her talk for hours on the telephone with her friends.)

- The consultant, after a confrontation with her mother to make the mother understand the psychological pain her egocentric attitude has caused her, does the following. She and the mother choose two ribbons: the daughter one color, the mother a different one. Standing, one in front of the other, they tie their ankles together, then their waists, wrists, necks. The consultant tells her mother, "You are you, I am I," words the mother repeats. Then, under the daughter's direction and with scissors, they cut the colored ribbons that bind their bodies. Once separated, they go to a place with fertile soil—a garden, a plaza, a park, or a forest—dig two adjacent holes and bury the ribbons without mixing them up (each color in its own cavity). In each hole, one woman plants a flowering plant: one plant chosen by the consultant, the other by the mother.

So that the consultant realizes the way in which she was possessed and frees herself, I recommend the following:

- The consultant enlarges a photograph of the mother's face, makes a mask of it with openings for each eye, then wears it in public, visiting establishments, friends, and relatives. That way her brain will understand what is seen by her mother's eyes. Afterward, the consultant should stand in front of her mother, remove the mask, rip it up, and hand the pieces to her mother saying, "Thank you for everything you gave me. Now I can be myself."

8. MOTHER-SON SYMBIOSIS

In societies influenced by the Christian religion, a man can aspire to be perfect; a woman cannot. She is only granted, as the highest achievement, to give birth to a perfect son. Upon having a son, some women, feeling incapable of succeeding socially by themselves, raise the child as if he were an extension and take over his mind. Through him, she acquires the perfection and power that the masculine society denies her. Metaphorically, feeling like her arms are cut off, she seizes the son's arms and acts through him. To be free of this symbiosis:

- The consultant, after a confrontation with his mother to make her understand the psychological pain that her possessive attitude has caused him, does the following. The mother should choose ribbon of a color that suits her. Standing up, his back to her chest, his ankles are tied to hers, his waist is tied to hers, his wrists are tied to hers, his neck is tied to hers. The consultant says to his mother, "You are you, I am me," and the mother repeats this phrase after him. Then she, with scissors, proceeds to cut the ribbons. Once the mother and son are separated, they go to an area of fertile soil (a garden, a plaza, a park, or a forest), and with four hands, they dig a hole and bury half of the pieces of ribbon. She plants there a little fruit tree. The consultant brings the other half of the ribbon to a temple and leaves it there at the base of a sculpture or a painting of a crucified Christ.

9. FATHER-SON SYMBIOSIS

Some egomaniacal fathers, who approach their sons as dangerous competitors, always have their sons under control, terrifying them with the future, telling them if they do not attain, financially, what they themselves have attained, they will suffer very badly, instilling, in this way, goals that do not belong to the son. Proving themselves to be insurmountable, these fathers fill their sons with anxiety, turning them into failures who hate money and who hate themselves for being fragile and cowardly. In order to break out of this constant paralysis, I advise the following:

- The consultant changes $20 into pennies (he will have a large package). He goes to a place where there are people feeding pigeons. He sits next to them and, calmly, as if they were seeds or breadcrumbs, begins to throw the coins at the birds. After having scattered at least ten handfuls of coins, the consultant returns home by foot, leaving coins along the way like a trail and emptying the bag until only one coin remains.

With the last coin, he makes an earring that will be hung from the right ear. The consultant goes to the father's home and, without offering any explanation, gives the father a round mirror (on which the consultant will have previously urinated and then washed off), together with a box, which had contained shoes but which now contains a large dildo. The consultant tells the father, "It is healthy to give but sick to force to receive. This is yours. I have mine. You will be grandfather to my sons and to my work, but not their father."

10. FATHER-DAUGHTER SYMBIOSIS

▶ The consultant goes toward her father dressed as a man, wearing very erotic undergarments. In front of him, she rips into pieces this suit (perhaps aided by a knife) until she is seminude and screaming, "I am not an unsuccessful man! I am not you! Look at me! Look at me for the first time exactly as I am! Are you capable of not converting me with your narcissistic dreams? Accept me! I am a woman! If you love me, come with me to bury these rags and then let me be free." If the father refuses, treating her like she's crazy, the consultant should not see him again for three years. If he accepts, the consultant dresses in a woman's suit and goes with her father to bury the torn suit and the provocative underwear along with a reproduction of a painting depicting Jupiter, Jehovah, or a dictator like Stalin or Pinochet, and then, above that, they should plant a rosebush.

11. INVASIVE MOTHER

When the father is absent (or indifferent), the mother can become invasive: infused with the mother-father role, overprotective of her children. Feeling herself indispensable, she is not able to bear her children's private life. When a consultant asks for advice for freedom from the mother, I reply that due to an atavistic instinct, it is impossible to eliminate the mother. Even if we stop seeing her forever or she has died, she continues to act from the darkness of the unconscious. But, yes, one can lessen the mother's intervention.

- To the mother, alive or dead—if the latter, she will be treated like a sacred idol—the consultant assigns a small table that will act as an altar and positions it in a corner of the house. There, the consultant places, in a silver frame, a photo of the mother that stays covered by a screen (so that the unconscious fully understands that the consultant has a prisoner). Behind it, the consultant places a lit candle, a vase with a flower, and a stick of incense. When the consultant eats at home, he sets up a little plate behind the photo-prisoner with a little bit of food: this way, the unconscious may well conclude that, since the mother is fed well, she cannot devour the consultant. The next day, the consultant gives the food that has been enshrined, whose essence has been devoured by the idol, to an animal, preferably, or, if that's not possible, he gathers the leftovers in an airtight container and, after forty days, buries them together with the already dried flowers that have been enshrined. The consultant should repeat this until he feels free of this invader.

But if the consultant, accepting his desire to kill her, insists on eliminating the mother completely, I advise the following:

- The consultant finds help from friends (a man and a woman) to accompany him to a deserted location to help dig a grave. Made up and disguised as the mother (shoes, clothes, wig), the consultant should lie down in the grave to be covered first with chocolates in the shape of gold coins and then with earth, leaving only the face exposed. The consultant should remain that way until he

> feels that the mother who invades his mind has dissolved. Once exhumed, the consultant should throw the clothes and others parts of the costume into the grave and be bathed by the two friends with blessed water, then eat seven chocolate coins and urinate in the mother's "tomb."

This way of rejecting the mother may seem excessive to the reader, but one must realize that to the whole, sane mother that one usually thinks of, other incomplete, insane mothers are added. We can say there are five types of mothers.

1. Murderous Mothers

They don't want to be mothers; they only want to be guaranteed that they are women. They can come from families where a secondary role was given to the female and praise was given to the male. There are legions of women in the world who suffer for being women: their families hope for a boy and not a girl. To satisfy the father, the daughter acts like a man; the mother, for her part, inculcates into the daughter that it is a disgrace to give birth and to become a slave to an unwanted offspring. She feels that apart from her brain, her body is prohibited. To live as a frustrated man, she rejects vaginal pleasure and in no way accepts becoming a mother. She gets inseminated in order to then abort. She needs to know that she is someone who can. She wants to be "someone who can" ultimately hide a rivalry with the father and, at the same time, an identification with the maternal image. The pregnancy calms for a time the sense of barrenness and her impotent desire to have a phallus. The self-hate, for feeling castrated, drives this woman to create a partnership with a man who hates his own mother and women in general.

Just as there are murderous mothers, there are murderous fathers who seek temporary relief from sexual tensions without any desire to procreate. The women who fall pregnant produce an unbearable nuisance.

2. Blocked Mothers

They want their bellies to swell but they don't want to give birth. Childish, they take advantage of their pregnancies to be surrounded by tenderness and care like a baby, which they lacked as a child. Being pregnant, becoming the center of the family's attention, allows them to satisfy affective needs. For nine months, they will feel happy, but immediately after delivery, they suffer from deep depression and perhaps hate their offspring for having deprived them of the care and attention that they obtained during pregnancy. They may produce acidic milk, causing diarrhea for the infants.

This type of woman will pair up with a man of similar childishness: accustomed to not being loved, he needs a pregnant woman; he projects himself onto the fetus. But he will feel anguish toward his unborn son and will feel indomitable jealousy; he will feel as if a younger brother has come to steal the maternal attention. Upon learning of the woman's pregnancy, he escapes.

Another kind of blocked mother is the result of families in which several generations of women have sacrificed their lives to have a great many children; some women even die during labor. These women will seek a man who believes himself a carrier of murderous semen. During pregnancy, he feels guilty and comes to hate his wife and the child she will deliver. As the months progress, the pregnant woman will experience great terror, oftentimes on the verge of aborting. She will need intensive care and months of bed rest. Her child will not be a messenger of life but of death. She will give birth, anesthetized and mostly by cesarean.

Another type of blocked mother is created when the mother is ashamed of being pregnant. For different reasons, neither her child nor the child's father agree with the family beliefs and plans: maybe she's a single mother or became pregnant through an act of incest or was inseminated by a man of another race. She believes the fruit of her belly is a sin or a betrayal. While she is pregnant, she leaves her home or she hides her belly, fearing that the child's birth will cause her to lose the love of her parents and relatives.

When a blocked mother gives birth—subtly acting as if her child were not completely born, trying to prevent him from developing his psychic autonomy—it is only possible at the price of a profound disturbance in the infant's development. This child may become psychotic or develop into a schizophrenic teenager or a maladjusted adult.

3. Dry Mothers

They are available for childbirth but they reject raising the infant who dared separate from their bodies; who only knows how to suck, nibble, and scream; and seeks her at every moment; and who distracts her from her sexual life and doesn't realize that she is an independent individual.

At one of my seminars in Barcelona, a married couple attended: the woman seven months pregnant. They told me that, by mutual agreement, she was going to follow a treatment of daily injections in order to stop milk from forming in her breasts. Breast feeding seemed disgusting to her. She added some other reasons, which, to the husband, seemed correct: she didn't want to deform her body, life was too short to sacrifice, she couldn't lose precious time away from her obligations as the manager of a company, having a child hang from her breast made her feel like an animal. It was clear that the woman in this couple acted as the enterprising man, the merchant, the family's breadwinner, working away from the home.

The man acted as the soul of the home devoted to the housework, preparing the food or giving the baby the bottle: a typical case of a couple with disrupted sexual identities. He doesn't know virility because he had a weak or absent father; he has an insatiable appetite for attention; he accepts that his wife is a mother, but he doesn't want her to be distracted by nurturing a rival. At every moment, he must be the center; his child will have a secondary role. They will raise an alcoholic, a smoker, a drug addict, or a sugar addict. A mother's milk cannot replace another mother's milk or that of any other animal. If breast feeding does not last the necessary time, the child may have difficulties talking; suffer from attacks of rage or chronic illness, intestinal pain, asthma, migraines, hypertension, panic attacks, and chronic fatigue; or spend a lifetime feeling unloved. Breast feeding is necessary during infancy to avoid these kinds of ill effects.

4. Possessive Mothers

This woman denies the man—an imitation of the hatred her mother suffered in the male world—and considers her child exclusively hers. She may give birth late and breast-feed more than is necessary. She will invade the child's psyche, suggesting that she is omnipotent. By iron will, she will keep the child in infantile limitations, turning the child into her audience. The child, not succeeding in becoming an adult, will fight her anxieties and powerlessness in order to be freed of this mother, who sometimes appears in the child's nightmares as a spider. The child will grow old trying to get the mother to really see her, achieving only being seen as a mirror that knows how to listen. The result of such an aberration takes the form of suicide, delusions of persecution, sterility, psychosis, and obsession with failure.

5. Whole, Healthy Mothers

Of a healthy mind and body, sexually satisfied, with balanced emotions, in a partnership of close collaboration, these mothers give birth, breast-feed, and raise their children in perfect harmony with nature. They will be conscious of the new child as not being the mother's viscera or organs, but rather the child is born as a necessity of the coming universe, in order to support new paths and become one more step toward evolution, which drives the human being toward immortality.

These mothers do not instill antiquated models of the past in the child but rather they only transmit the values of their ancestors; they are guided by the child, considering him the teacher, giving him that which he indicates he needs, and not forcing the goals of the family trap, which could paralyze the child or divert him from his essential self. The child never becomes the sole possession for the healthy mother, who shares the child with her partner and with the world. The healthy mother will not say "do this" without showing the child the best possible options, giving the child the opportunity to choose. These mothers know how to adapt themselves to the necessities of the baby: breast-feeding for the time needed, supporting the baby with loving arms, and cuddling him sweetly. This experience allows the child to, from the breast, feel real and to be that which the possibility of doing and receiving will, before long, give him.

(If the reader has suffered some from any of the first four mothers, he or she may find relief in number 79, "Birth Massage," pg. 128.)

12. MOTHERS WHO CRITICIZE BY TELEPHONE

There are mothers who, living separated from their daughters, often call them by telephone. Suffering from perfectionism, they develop an egotistical spirit. They feel themselves right about everything, projecting onto their daughters the defects that they cannot accept in themselves. Each time these mothers communicate with their daughters, the mothers cannot stop criticizing them. If an absent father is added to this, and the child can only count on maternal love, every harsh word wounds the child in a most intimate way. In this case, I recommend the following:

- Make a heart out of red cork to put next to the telephone. (The consultant must prohibit the mother from calling the cell phone.) Each time the consultant receives one of the mother's verbal assaults, the consultant must stick a dart into the cork. When the heart is full, the consultant should count the darts without removing them and buy an equal number of chocolates wrapped in metallic red paper. If there are fifty darts, there will be fifty chocolates. The consultant mails the heart pinned with darts and circled with chocolates in a gift box together with a pink card on which will be written, "For you, dear Mother, because I love you. I forgive you for the pain your criticism has caused me."

13. MOURNING AN ABORTION

However much an abortion is justified, it leaves painful marks on the woman's soul. To the organic wound, the shock of the operation is added, which has been suffered without the presence of the man who is responsible for the fertilization. An abortion, in our masculine society, which generally aids the male in eluding responsibility, basically involves the woman and her fetus. Many times, in the deep recesses, the woman hauls around an abysmal sadness for this child whom she will never see grow up. In order to perform bereavement so that the consultant feels relief, I recommend this act:

- Concentrating deeply, the consultant should choose a small fruit to represent the fetus. She undresses and places the fruit atop her stomach, wraps a flesh-colored bandage around her body four times—holding it in the place where the abortion was suffered—and asks a good friend or lover to, little by little, cut the bandage with a scalpel and remove the fruit. During this metaphysical operation, the consultant will let her grief and rage surface in the form of complaints, cries, or insults. Then the consultant leaves the fruit in a pretty box that she has decorated.

  At once, accompanied by her associate, the consultant, with a black pebble (a mortuary symbol of accumulated pain) in her mouth, will go to a nice spot to bury this symbolic casket. She digs in the earth with her hands, helped by a man: a collaboration she did not have in the past. She spits the black pebble into the hole. The man, who will have put a red candy in his mouth, kisses the consultant and slides the candy onto her tongue (the symbol of rebirth of life). They put a plant in the little grave, and if it is possible, they make love together. If this companion is only a good friend, they go to a café for something nice to eat.

In cases in which the consultant has suffered multiple abortions, increase the number of fruits and put as many black pebbles in the mouth as corresponds to the number of abortions. That way, in only one act, the consultant can fulfill this gloomy ceremony for all of the sacrificed lives.

14. NOSTALGIA FOR HOMELAND

The most painful traumas are caused by the loss of a loved one. Those are followed in intensity by traumas caused by the loss of homeland or personal territory. I once heard a Mapuche healer in Chile tell a North American tourist, "You aren't anyone. You are a man without a country." On another occasion, a French couple came to me for a consultation; these two were raised and married in Algeria. Many years earlier they were kicked out of their country with their four-year-old daughter. They arrived in Paris by force to start their lives over in a city they always considered cold, distant, and ruthless. For years they repeated, in front of their daughter, "This is no life. In Algeria we were happy. In Paris one cannot live." The couple found their daughter dead at ten years old one morning when, the day before, this child had been in perfect health.

For the consultant who misses his birthplace, to cure this nostalgia, I recommend:

- The consultant requests someone to send ten pounds of the earth from the yearned-for land. Each day, for a half hour, having placed the earth in an open container, the consultant places his feet in this earth while he meditates, reads, or watches television. The consultant takes one of these "footbaths" each time an attack of nostalgia appears.

I also recommend, for those who immigrated, to travel to one's birthplace and plant a tree there or as close as possible.

15. TAKING POSSESSION OF A TERRITORY

In order to mark their territory, animals urinate. Some consultants who have changed houses or who have opened an office or a business do not feel good, and for hidden reasons, they don't acclimatize to this new place. To make them feel that the environment is favorable and that it truly belongs to them, I recommend:

- The consultant urinates in a container and, with an eyedropper, wanders around the new space depositing three drops of urine in every corner of each room.

16. SEPARATED PARENTS

So that a child's character can grow in a balanced way, parents must understand the child intellectually: that is to say that the parents do not express contradictory concepts of life in front of the child; that the parents are united emotionally, they treat one another with respect, care, and admiration; that the parents desire one another sexually, and they express satisfaction in this regard; and that they do not make the child a participant in their financial anxieties, making sure that they will always be able to give the child what he or she needs without anything essential missing.

The children of parents who do not love them, who argue constantly, who divorce, or who turn the children over to the care of an aunt or the grandparents feel that their personalities are divided, without a united goal. Even if they live at a good economic level, they live devoid of protection, without the ability to believe they are loved by their partners. For this kind of consultant, I advise:

- The consultant tattoos a sun on the sole of the right foot (symbol of the cosmic father) and a moon on the sole of the left foot (symbol of the cosmic mother). That way, each time the consultant walks, she feels parental support.

  The consultant can also experience mother-father unity by walking with headphones. At the same time, the consultant listens through the left side to a song sung by a woman and through the right, a song sung by a man.

For the consultant who was abandoned or rejected, I advise:

- The consultant tapes a photograph of the mother on a bottle of virgin olive oil and a photograph of the father on a bottle of liquor. If the parent is unknown, the consultant can use the image of someone admirable. Each night, before bed, the consultant puts seven drops of this oil and seven drops of this alcohol into a small wine glass and drinks it in one swig. This way, the unconscious will feel nourished by the mother-father presence, and after some time, the feeling of abandonment will disappear.

For consultants with some artistic talent who feel their personalities are split in two, I advise:

- Helped by a friend of the opposite sex or by his partner, the consultant paints the right half of the body gold and the left half silver—in this way uniting in the body the two symbolic colors for the sun and moon. The consultant should paint or draw with pencils or paintbrushes—gold in one hand, silver in the other—a self-portrait, healthy and smiling, as an infant. After finishing the painting and signing his first name and including the father's and mother's last names, the consultant (still with the body painted silver and gold) should photograph the painting and send it by Internet to as many friends and relatives as possible.

For a very nervous consultant who complains of not being able to calm down (agitation produced because her parents never stopped quarreling), I advise:

- The consultant visits her parents, carrying a few yards of leather strapping. The consultant tells them, "I will never have serenity if I don't see you two agree." She puts the parents face-to-face and ties them together with the leather strap. The consultant observes them for a while, until she can express her grief, fears of abandonment, and anger, then she cuts the strap and gives part to the mother and part to the father. The three go to a forest, dig a hole, and, together, plant three flowering potted plants: one chosen by the mother, another by the father, the third by the consultant.

17. ECZEMA

At times, due to issues of a psychological nature, skin problems can arise. These are, actually, a request for caresses not obtained during childhood. These problems indicate that the sufferer lacked the needed care from some of his or her loved ones. These allergic reactions may be due to requests or rejections. To a consultant who has suffered an outbreak on the left side, I ask, "On what side does your spouse sleep?" One consultant said the left, and I advised him to have his wife sleep on the right side. He did this. The outbreak disappeared on the left side but appeared on the right side. This is a case of rejection due to lack of proper communication. The anger and grudges that are not verbalized can transform into eczema.

As for the needed attention, a celebrated French guru consulted with me after his recent marriage to a much younger (she could have been his daughter) disciple whose mother had raised her alone (absent father). This mother suffered from her daughter's departure and from her daughter's marriage to a man better suited, in age, to be her father. She was not able to express her jealousy and rage toward this generous and impeccable guru, however, and eczema manifested in the palms of both hands. The guru asked me for advice and I recommended:

- The consultant and the young wife, in front of the mother, should spit into a bit of green clay powder and make a paste with it, then apply it to the mother's infected palms. Satisfied with the couple's tenderness, the mother healed.

It is best for the consultant to find two loving people (a man and a woman), in agreement, with whom to make this green clay and saliva paste and who will both apply it to the eczema or the eruption.

18. AVOID BEING SPELLBOUND BY A MORE POWERFUL MIND

The human mind, finding itself face-to-face with a more powerful mind, tends to forget itself, relinquishing its will to the whim of the stronger mind. In order to advance on the path of consciousness, it is necessary for us to build up strength of mind and lose the fear of observing ourselves even though our thoughts, feelings, and desires disgust us. When, instead of concentrating on subjective events (with the intention of freeing herself from an untrustworthy personality formed by the family, society, or culture), the consultant is enthralled by another person's ego, who takes advantage of her psychological weakness and absorbs her life energy, she should do as follows:

- The consultant puts a raw pork chop wrapped in aluminum foil in her pocket. Each time she feels like she is beginning to forget herself, the consultant puts her hand in the pocket and clutches the silver package. This absurd act of clutching a pork chop sends the consultant back to herself, freeing the consultant of an invasive influence.

  But, if after seeing this powerful person, and in spite of the pork chop, the consultant continues feeling trapped by the person's influence, the consultant should write the person's name with china ink on blotting paper like this:

  ALFRED
  ALFRE
  ALFR
  ALFR
  ALF
  AL
  A

  Next to it, do the same with the person's last name. Fold the blotting paper in four parts and burn it in the flame of a black candle.

19. BAD LUCK

If a streak of bad things overwhelms the consultant and convinces him of his bad luck, after exploring what he feels so guilty about (which drives the consultant to punish himself so), I advise the practice of a "cleanse," following the recipe of the Mexican healers for freeing oneself of injurious influences. Even if the consultant doesn't believe in it, his unconscious will accept this imaginary healing as real.

- The consultant puts two liters of water on to warm in a saucepan and adds three handfuls of coarse salt. He then soaks a bunch of parsley in this mixture and rubs it over the whole body, beginning on the left side. He repeats this twice daily: once in the morning and once at night. After each rub, the consultant puts the parsley in the empty saucepan, sprinkles it with alcohol, lights it on fire, and throws the ashes down the toilet. He should do this successively for seven days.

20. AGORAPHOBIA

When a person is not able to leave the house, suffering from an irrational fear of the exterior world, his unconscious identifies the home with the interior of the maternal womb. The expectant mother's feelings are transmitted to the fetus and remain there recorded into cellular memory. If the mother fears giving birth because she considers the exterior world dangerous and wants to keep the child in her belly forever, the child receives the order: do not be born (an order that remains in effect throughout all of life). If the child exits into a vast space, he is born disobeying the maternal wishes. The punishment—rather than to be destroyed by the outside world—will be to stop being loved by the mother. To the consultant afflicted by agoraphobia, I recommend:

- The consultant solicits the help of four couples who will call on the consultant at her home. The consultant will be placed nude in a sleeping bag and provided with a sharp knife. Her helpers will firmly close the bag, and enclosed like that, they will take the consultant to a public place.

  Upon being deposited there, the consultant should, with the knife, cut a long slit in the bag and, slowly, begin to come out, imagining that she is being born. As the consultant emerges, the eight collaborators, holding hands, circle the consultant while singing a song from a children's game. When the consultant has completely emerged, each couple pours over the "newborn" a liter of blessed water. They dress her with new clothes and, including her in the game, the collaborators turn the consultant around inside the circle eight times. The consultant releases and breaks free from this circle, walking backward. Then, screaming her new name, the consultant runs around the public space in a big circle.

Afterward, everyone goes to a café to have a refreshing drink and eat something sweet. The consultant should send the sleeping bag and the knife, wrapped like a gift, plus a box of chocolates to her mother. If the mother is dead, the consultant should take the package to her tomb.

This is a card from a Spanish consultant:

Sunday, July 6, 2006, at 12:00 in the Plaza Mayor in Valladolid, I followed your instructions to a tee. In the sleeping bag, I was panicked: I wanted to cry and scream. When I got out of it, and they poured water over my head, the space quit terrorizing me. I ran, I jumped, I screamed with arms opened around the whole plaza, feeling happiness. . . . During the week, I felt confused, and although a bit of fear remains, I have already gone out alone twice.

If the consultant doesn't have friends or the means to gather together eight people, I recommend this:

- During the house confinement, the consultant should always urinate in a potty chair rather than the toilet. When the consultant has acquired the habit of using this container, each time he tries to go outdoors, he should carry the potty chair in a bag. At the first sign of anxiety, he goes to the restroom in a café and uses the potty then empties it in the toilet. This act turns the outside territory into personal space and, in this way, ends the consultant's anxiety.

21. CLAUSTROPHOBIA

Fear of staying in enclosed spaces is normal among all animals. The loss of freedom means death or the possibility of being devoured. In the unconscious of the claustrophobic person or of close relatives or ancestors, there are childhood experiences of painful or maybe deadly confinement. If the consultant is brave and is ready to bear her anxiety for a few moments, she can be healed. Instead of fleeing the panic, she should deeply surrender to it. I recommend:

- First, the consultant must find a coffin. Then, accompanied by six charitable people (three men and three women) ready to fulfill a therapeutic act, she goes to a place that is near an enclosed area that is upsetting. There, the consultant encloses herself nude in the coffin whose top has a hole to allow her to breathe. The six people carry the coffin and place it in this feared area. The consultant remains in the enclosed space as long as possible and then asks the friends to remove the top. The six people do so and, without removing the consultant from the coffin, begin to cover her body with honey. Then, letting out hoarse grunts, they begin to lick the consultant entirely. At the end of this, the consultant leaves her enclosure. She dresses with new clothes and kicks against the walls exclaiming, "Nothing can lock me in; my soul does not have limits!" Enclosed spaces, from this point on, will appear spacious.

If the consultant does not have friends or the means of gathering six persons, I recommend the following:

- The consultant should memorize by heart text that builds her trust in a supreme consciousness—eternal and infinite—to free her psyche from the anguish. The consultant, feeling enclosed, removes the right shoe and, propping it strongly against her head, she recites aloud:

Without beginning, without end,
origin of all my gestures,
light that pierces my shadows,
breath that revives the dust,
epitome of all time,
I am with you,
I trust you,
if I accept you in me,
nothing confines me.

22. BULIMIA

The mind (with its language of ideas) aspires to knowledge; the heart (with its language of feelings) aspires to love; the genitals (with their language of desires) aspire to satisfaction; the body (with its language of need) aspires to security. These four energy centers, which, when unfulfilled, invite all types of neuroses in the individual, are connected to each other and can be trained to communicate with each other. An open intellect can understand what a sublime emotion is; an open heart can give us knowledge; the satisfaction that sex cannot obtain, the body manages to get.

With bulimia (a never-satisfied urge to eat), due to childhood trauma probably caused by a competitive mother who has inhibited in her daughter incestuous urges toward the father or toward her, the consultant faults the obtainment of sexual pleasure and replaces sexual caresses with an insatiable desire to eat. (Note: The recommendations for healing are not the same for a man and a woman.)

- The consultant, who satisfies sexual desire through the mouth, should, each time her lust impels her to devour food, insert a piece of it into her vagina, which she should keep in the vagina until she is finished eating. In this way, her unconscious will understand that sexual satisfaction is allowed. The food in her vagina will be taken out and kept in a plastic bag. When the bag is full, it should be taken to fertile grounds and emptied in a hole and flowers should be planted.

If the consultant is a man, it is very possible that his bulimia grows out of a cannibal urge to eat his mother. If he had a competitive father who did not want to share the woman with his son, the consultant, with his unsatisfied wishes to nurse, will transform all food into a symbol of his mother, and he will not quit eating until bursting—never able to satisfy himself.

▶ I recommend the male consultant sculpt a carving of his mother, using eight pounds of almond paste. He should color it with food coloring. Each time he eats food, he should, at the end, like a dessert, eat a piece of the sculpture. In this way, he will fulfill his cannibal impulses. At the same time, he should hire a wet nurse and nurse from her breasts twice a day while otherwise fasting: once in the morning and once at night. Little by little the intensity of his bulimia will wane.

I received this request for help: "I have high cholesterol since my separation from my spouse seventeen years ago, and I am unable to find a diet without fat. Can you give me a psychomagic remedy?" My response:

▶ From a butcher, buy a pound of animal fat (without any bones). Cook it on the grill and eat only this (breakfast, lunch, snack, dinner). Do this on Friday. Repeat this for four Fridays (4 times 4 equals 16, the number of years of separation). Then you will never be able to eat fat again. Once you have finished eating the pound of fat, rub your mouth with a photograph of the person from whom you are separated. At the end of four Fridays, bury this photo and plant a lemon tree above it.

23. ANOREXIA

Anorexia, the lack of normal desire to eat, is an illness in which the affected woman (the percentage of men is much lower) is convinced by a distorted and delusional perception that she is fat even when her weight drops below a healthy level. Therefore, she reduces the ingestion of food, and she gradually diminishes in weight until she puts her life at risk.

This sick person's family must put her under medical treatment.

However, to heal there has to be a desire to heal, and the anorexic doesn't want to eat at all: her delirium makes her reject all help. In this case, psychomagic is not used to cure the illness (which belongs to the field of medicine) but to give the sick person the desire to cure herself.

Wanting to study Mapuche medicine, I traveled to Temuco in the south of Chile to attend a *machitún,* a healing ritual with a big congregation of tribes around a track where they submit to a game similar to hockey that they call *chueca* (crooked). The game was opened with five *machis* (the tribes' chief healers). I had the opportunity to speak with the most respected of these *machis.*

"What do you want to know?" he asked me.

"I want to know how you heal," I said.

"The first thing to find out is who is the owner of the illness."

"The owner?"

"All illnesses have an owner. If they don't, they die abandoned. I need to discuss with their owners the price of the healing ceremony."

In the case of anorexia, the sick person (unwilling to begin her healing) must be prepared by the "owners," which could be her relatives—preferably her mother or father. Above all, they must realize that they are in large part responsible for the illness of their daughter, either because they have removed her from the home or instilled in her a morality that requires a rapturous purity (which is to say, the rejection of sexual pleasure) or because they abused her when she was little or the mother suffered with obesity or they divorced or one of them died prematurely. One might add to this that perhaps, overwhelming her with criticism or destroying her self-esteem, they locked her up in the clan, thereby destroying her social skills and her communication with the environment.

This hate of the flesh has its roots in the ancestors' religious concepts that considered female sexuality a manifestation of the devil. One of the first recognized cases of anorexia is that of the mystic and tertiary of the Dominican Order Catherine of Siena (1347–1380) who, when she was seven, made the promise to dedicate her chastity and life to God. At a young age, she entered the order already underweight. She shut herself in her room and abused herself by not eating. She died soon after. Her prestige moved quickly through religious circles: fasting was a means for the spirit to triumph over the flesh. To go without eating (without sexual relations) was considered a sign of saintliness.

These absurd religious ideas are transmitted, overlapping most of the time, from generation to generation, and they originate from delusional wishes for perfection, contempt for sexual pleasure, exaltation of spiritual purity, and hatred toward the body.

Anorexia does not appear in families with few economic resources. Not eating when there is nothing to eat is not the same as not eating when there is food. The sick person is surrounded by care in an environment void of grave financial issues. Psychologists recommend putting the sufferer in a climate of understanding, kindness, and good manners in order to gradually recuperate her self-esteem and love for life.

In this case of anorexia, and with good results, I dared advise a psychomagic act totally opposite to official methods.

▶ Without the anorexic knowing, I met with her parents and I convinced them to arrange a theatrical event hiring three male

> actors—in appearance, the most aggressive possible—to stage a fake kidnapping. The mother took the daughter out shopping. In the middle of the street, two actors got out of the car and threatened the two women with pistols, forcing the daughter to get into the car. The third actor drove. The actors gagged her, covered her head with a bag, and, after driving around town for an hour, took her to a dark room and locked her in it, with only a dirty old mattress and a pail in which to urinate and defecate. Before leaving her there, they threw her down and stripped her naked. For three days, without speaking to her, they offered her, in a dog bowl, the low-calorie food she was addicted to in her fight to lose weight.
>
> Each time the food came with a dead cockroach in it. On the fourth day, the actors entered her prison with a video camera and threatened to rape her if she didn't let them film her begging her parents to pay the high ransom that her captors were demanding. Two days later, the actors told her that the ransom had been paid. They gagged her, covered her head with the bag, and brought her back, driving around again for an hour, to finally left her, naked as she was before, at the door of her house.

The shock this fake abduction produced in the girl caused her to be disgusted by her food regimen and her skeletal body and to show gratitude toward her family for having gathered so much money for her ransom, forgetting her grudges for not having felt cared for. Finally, she readily agreed, with the desire to heal herself, to submit to a diet under medical supervision.

24. FAILURE

The consultant who sent me the following e-mail got drunk at a party that ended in an orgy, and a stranger got her pregnant:

> According to my mother, I do not have the right to exist. Therefore, I don't have the right to create either or to conceive or to complete any constructive act. My book, a collection of photographs of spiritual teachers, has not been published in spite of all the energy I employed to present it to editors. Everything I do, my mother hides or destroys. She has thrown my writings in the garbage just as she did my dictionary of philosophy. She has trashed my negatives, screaming how she hates my photographs. She ousted me from her life by sending this message through one of my friends: "I never want to hear about you again." When I lived with her, I only had the right to disappear or fulfill the role of a simple puppet that she imposed on me. I was raised with constant guilt for being what I am. I write without any hope. I don't believe anyone can help me.

There are people who, in spite of participating in all kinds of therapy, cannot free themselves from the feeling that they have failed in their professions, in love, with the family, in their projects. They have lost hope that something will accord them value. Life appears unbearable to them, but according to these people, because of cowardice, they cannot commit suicide. It is difficult with words to convince a person who totally negates any consolation whatsoever: what has happened is that she has ceased to love herself and now despises herself. If a consultant is in this state, I say this: just as the person believes, it is impossible to cure the person. The only thing left to do is die to be reborn a new person. I therefore recommend:

- The consultant, if she doesn't have friends, hires a couple of collaborators (a woman and a man). They go to a nice place away from the city and dig a shallow pit. The night before, the consultants reads her own funeral speech, recounting her life passages. She then undresses and wraps herself in a sheet. Lying in the pit, the collaborators cover her with dirt, leaving the consultant's face uncovered so she can breathe. In this immobilized state, she surrenders to the nothingness.

Looking at the stars, the consultant should let go of everything until no interest ties her to the character she was. The consultant will remain in the pit surrounded by ten burning candles as long as possible, and when she sincerely feels it, she should say, "I want to be reborn!" The collaborators then dig the consultant out, wash her with blessed water, and give her clean, white clothes.

Once the consultant is dressed, she allows her new name to come to mind. She then writes her previous name on a piece of parchment paper and, together with the old clothes and the candles, buries it in the pit. On returning to the city, the consultant will burn a dry tree (or a dry tree branch) to which, prior to the burial, the consultant will have nailed pictures of all family members (grandparents, parents, uncles, and siblings); if photos do not exist, the consultant should use a drawing or a painting of look-alikes. She then takes the ashes, dissolves them in a liter of virgin olive oil, covers her whole body with this paste, and then lies down on the floor to sleep.

Upon waking, the consultant showers by soaping and rinsing seven times in a row. She dresses in new clothes. Then she gathers up all her old clothes and donates them to a charity. She washes down the floors, walls, and ceilings where she lives with blessed water. She changes the furniture, buys new tableware, and, with a hammer, shatters the old. She replaces her tablecloth and cutlery. And, finally, the consultant prints business cards with her new name.

I received this other request for help:

I am lost, without work, without home, living with friends who at this point are tired of me. My life is a big chain of ruptures: my father killed himself, I don't speak with my mother, I am incapable of paying my bills, and I spend money compulsively. I married someone HIV positive, to help him, and now even he can't stand me. I am bisexual. I am addicted to cocaine. Things get worse and worse. Sooner or later, people end up despising me or me them, which condemns me to a terrible loneliness. I am very sad. I need help. I am on a ship with no direction, without wind. The groceries are gone, love is a series of impossible passions, I am afraid. All joy in existence is lost. How can I recover it?

My response:

- Eat as much as you can. When this is digested, and you need to go to the bathroom, defecate in a potty chair. Then rub this excrement all over your naked body. Get dressed in torn and dirty clothes, go out onto the street to beg, stinking like that, for three hours, and then go to your mother's home, demanding to use her bathroom. Carry with you a package of clean clothes. When you exit, clean and well dressed, pitch the stinky clothes in a public dumpster saying, "Trash return to the trash. I, life, return to life." Force yourself to laugh aloud and go to a friend's house (or where you currently live) with a bouquet of roses. If you are able to do this, you will recoup the happiness of living.

25. NICOTINE ADDICTION

When a consultant is prey to an addiction, it is impossible to detach from it if he does not wish to do so. And when the consultant does wish to do so, he needs enormous willpower to achieve it. After first trying to reduce as much as possible the daily quantity of cigarettes, the consultant should achieve this in twenty-two days by following this exercise:

- The consultant sleeps only four hours each night. Placing a vessel full of water and rubber gloves near his bed, the consultant goes to bed at midnight and wakes up with an alarm clock at four in the morning. Upon opening his eyes, the consultant covers his head with a sheet and, sticking an arm out of one side, takes the wet rubber gloves and rubs them over his entire body. Then, covered like that, he leaves the little bit of remaining water to evaporate. He gets up and takes a cold shower. The consultant should feel full of new energy. With a thick, felt-tip pen, he writes on one side of a packet of cigarettes, "No!" and on the other side, "I can!" He eats at a Japanese restaurant and keeps the chopsticks to cut them into pieces the size of a cigarette, then puts them in a package with a little bottle full of blessed water. Each time the consultant wants to smoke, he takes out a little piece of stick, wets it in the blessed water, and sucks it until the desire passes.

If this vice reigns in such a way that, in spite of these efforts, the consultant still feels incapable of quitting, the consultant should demonstrate to his unconscious how harmful the habit is. To accomplish this, he should do the following:

- The consultant makes wax dolls of his loved ones. On each doll, he glues some hair and fingernails of his loved ones. Each time during the day that the consultant smokes, he draws a line in a booklet. Upon returning to his home, the consultant counts the lines then sticks pins with black heads into the dolls: one pin for each cigarette smoked. Even if the consultant is a rational person, free of superstitions, this act of witchcraft will be accepted by the unconscious as real harm to loved ones. Little by little, sequestered by guilt, the consultant will quit smoking. So then, after removing the pins and burying them in a potted plant that will remain in the consultant's home, he melts each doll into heart shapes and sends them as gifts to loved ones, putting each one in the center of a box of chocolates.

26. HEROIN ADDICTION

For a consultant to liberate himself from the need to inject this pain-killer into his blood, the consultant needs a superhuman will: it is impossible to do this by reason. It is necessary to employ measures that blame the unconscious in such a way that the prisoner of this evil habit not only understands but feels in the depths of his spirit that destroying himself is as harmful as destroying the lives of others.

- I recommend the consultant buys, to begin with, twelve cage birds and twelve white rats. Each time the consultant goes to inject himself, he should squeeze in his right hand a bird and in the left hand a rat, applying enough pressure to break their bones. The consultant will store the cadavers in an airtight, transparent jar and let them accumulate until his consciousness, sick of seeing the killing of defenseless beings, prevents him from any further injecting.

27. ALCOHOLISM

To relieve a person suffering from alcoholism is a team effort that members of Alcoholics Anonymous know very well. Therefore, the following psychomagic act only aims to improve the relations between an alcoholic and the person he lives with. (See also case number 28.)

- It is necessary, in a corner of a room, that the consultant make an altar on which is placed a statue of the Virgin Mary with a child in her arms. Next to her, a bottle of the alcohol preferred by the consultant afflicted by this addiction. The consultant glues on the bottle a photograph of his mother. Each night, he lights two sticks of incense at the altar and puts on the altar a glass with two fresh roses in it. At bedtime, the friend of the person addicted to alcohol will give him a back and chest massage with the liquor from the bottle on the altar. Thus, the poison acts as an antidote, acquiring—

besides a sacred meaning—the quality of balance for the absence of maternal tenderness in early childhood, thereby decreasing the consultant's lack of self-esteem and guilt and improving his relationship with the one who gives him the massages.

As with the case of bulimia (see case number 22), I recommend the consultant hire a wet nurse and suckle twice daily while fasting: once in the morning and once at night. Little by little, the intensity of the thirst for alcohol will decrease.

28. LIVING WITH AN ADDICT

An alcoholic, a morphine addict, a gambling addict, and any other kind of addict are incapable of loving another person normally. Healthy love is an equal exchange between two winners. Addicts, however, whirling around themselves, establish partnerships in which the addict is the "winner" and whoever accompanies him is the "loser." The addict demands care and sacrifice and has endless expectations (like children) and is incapable, however, of giving back.

The person who is attached to the addict does not love herself. The person's self-esteem is so low that she only believes she has value when she sacrifices herself to helping others. But this person lies to herself, saying the self-destroyer appreciates her and that, when he is finally freed from the addiction or vice, he will love her. Ultimately, having been a child not loved by her parents, this person repeats the childhood suffering, trying by all means to earn a love that will never be given. Even though she knows she is wasting her life, motivated by a compassion that conceals the painful desire to be acknowledged, the person may be incapable of cutting off this insane relationship. I advise, therefore, the consultant to say this to the addicted person:

- For a woman: "You are sick. I am not your wife or your lover but your nurse. From now on, I will always be at your side in a nurse's uniform, and I will accompany you everywhere we go in this uniform—whether it is to a restaurant, the cinema, the grocery store, the homes of our friends, and so forth." The consultant will gather all of her clothes into a trunk and dress in a nurse's uniform, wearing around her neck a locket with a photograph of the addict's mother in it. For a man: In this case, each time the consultant is with the addict, he will dress in the nurse's uniform and will wear a locket around his neck with a photograph of the addict's father in it.

29. DEATH OF A BABY

"God gives. God takes. Blessed be God!" "We won't think of his absence. We will be thankful for the time he gave joy to our lives." "The divine drop returned to its ocean of origin." "Her soul has dissolved into eternal happiness." "The dead no longer suffer." As wise as they are, these phrases or ideas said by parents who have lost a child do not console the parents. The fact of burying a body, or of cremating it before spreading the ashes, is felt by the unconscious as a return to matter, to the coldness of the earth's darkness. To complete the farewell ceremony to add spiritual relief, this is my recommendation:

- The parents frame a photograph of the deceased child and fasten to it four or more white balloons filled with gas so that the photograph floats up and is lost in the sky.

This same ceremony can be used for other difficult deaths, attaching a photograph of an adult relative or a pet.

30. BORN AFTER THE DEATH OF A SIBLING

It is important to know that our birth has been an anticipated event; that we wish to be within that family and not in another. If a child is born after the death of a sibling, and her parents name her after the late sister, this means that she has come to replace the other, which compels this person to not be herself. Without realizing it, she lives up to being dead. This becomes more obvious when the child is dubbed, for example, Reynold or Renalda, which means "return to life," or else the parents give the child an initial or a syllable from the name of the departed like: RObert turns into ROdney, BErtha to BEatrice, ALexander to ALbert, MARtha to MARia, ANnie to MelANie or MirANda. When the consultant becomes aware of "not being," I recommend:

- The consultant procures a pound of almond paste and, at midnight, lies down nude and spreads the paste like a second skin over the chest and stomach. She falls asleep that way, lying down with the eyes toward the sky. When the consultant wakes up—after ten minutes or a couple of hours or whatever duration of sleep—she should sculpt with the almond paste a doll that represents the dead child. Then the consultant should paint it with edible vegetable dye, put it in a pretty box, and give it as a gift to the mother, or the father, or both, requesting to have coffee or tea with them as well as petitioning them to eat a piece of the doll (the consultant will not eat it). If the parents are dead, the consultant deposits half the doll on one grave and the other half on the other grave and says, "So that the dead devour the dead." Then the consultant changes her name, not legally but by way of a mailing asking relatives and friends to use the new name when addressing the consultant.

The consultant should also carry out this act if the parents named her after a relative who died of tragic circumstances, for example, an aunt who committed suicide.

If we realize we have committed an error by giving a child a name that carries problems, and we decide to change it, we should be careful not to cause the dissolution of personality: the child's name has turned into his territory; to depart sharply is like leaving the child homeless. To avoid this, I recommend:

- The parents show the child a little silver chest (for a little girl) or gold (for a little boy) and say, "My child, little birds live in a nest. Names, like little birds, have a place for shelter. This little chest is the nest for your name." The parents should open the chest and take out a piece of vellum upon which is written the child's birth name. "In this chest, you can leave your name, and that way, you will never lose it. You can put it in your room. This is the name that fit you because you were small. Now you are big, and we are going to call you by a new, beautiful name that will give you powers that correspond to what you are." Then offer the child a little marzipan bar on which, with sugar letters, the new name is written. "On this bar is written your new name; eat it. That way it will enter into your body, and it will be yours forever." At the same time, uniting their voices, the father and mother will read the new name and wait for the child to eat the sweet bar. Then they hug the child and congratulate him or her. "From now on, we will call you this. When you remember your old name, you only have to open the little chest and speak with it, telling it you love it and that you haven't forgotten it. Then tell it to continue sleeping."

31. GIVE THE FEELINGS OF OTHERS BACK TO THEM

The neurons of an infant brain, like mirrors, have the ability to reflect and store the parents' feelings. We are raised feeling misery that is not our own. Also, due to the desire to belong to them and to be loved by them, we reproduce our ancestors' illnesses. They, in turn, cannot see our individuality, and they turn us into their extensions. The great-grandfather's name (and his occupation, too) can be transmitted to the grandfather, father, and grandson, and in this name, the ancestor's destiny is contained. Many times, by joining the clan, depression, a failure, a tumor, and so forth are transmitted from one relative to the other. In cases such as these, I recommend:

- The consultant should first say, "This wrong does not belong to me. It belongs to [this or that relative]!" Then the consultant finds one or more (according to the level of trouble) balls from the game boules and paints them black (for a tumor or depression) or gray (for financial or emotional failure) or dark green (for lack of self-esteem). The consultant should always carry the heavy ball(s) in a backpack except when he bathes or sleeps. At the end of seven days, the consultant should send the ball(s), wrapped as a Christmas gift, to whomever this invasive feeling or illness belongs with a beautiful bouquet of flowers and a card with the following inscription: "This belongs to you. I am returning it because it was never mine."

A famous sculptor who fulfilled every one of her life's desires (prosperity, success, healthy family) was afflicted with attacks of depression that included the desire to commit suicide by a bullet to the head. This feeling was not hers but her mother's, who never accomplished her artistic vocation. I recommended that she sculpt a marble pistol, paint it black, carry it in a sack for a lunar month, and, at the beginning of her menstruation, send this pistol as a gift to her mother with a box of chocolates in the shape of a heart.

32. LETTING GO OF CHILDHOOD SUFFERING

Sometimes parents cannot satisfy their child's wishes; for example: the family is forced to leave a home the child loves; or due to divorce, the child is separated from a parent; or the parent doesn't have enough money to give the child what he asks for; or a grandparent dies. This causes great distress for the child who may shut herself up, lose her appetite, cease to smile, and so forth. To resolve these situations, I recommend:

- The parents should make a doll that looks like the child with an excessively sad face. The parents tell the child, "This is your sadness. We are going to take it out. We are going to take it to the cinema [or to whatever place pleases the distressed child]." The child should take the doll in his arms. During the film, the doll should sit in the seat next to the child. At the ice-cream parlor, the child can rub the doll's mouth with the ice-cream cone. Filled with joy at the end of the day, the child, having carried his "sorrow" around all day, attaches enough helium balloons to the doll so that, when released, the doll is lost in the high altitudes. "See! Your sorrow is going to the sky. The angels are in charge of her. Now you can be happy."

33. LETTING GO OF HARMFUL IDEAS

Our brains tend to fulfill predictions. The words are recorded in our neurons and are turned into orders. Children are shaped according to their parents' views. If the parents do not recognize the children and project onto these little ones what they wish them to be, without accepting who they truly are, the children will grow up feeling empty. They form the habit of negative self-talk, and the more they repeat these impairments, the more they fulfill them. To the consultants with certain negative self-concepts ("I am a failure," "I'm good for nothing," "Men/Women hate me," "I will never be rich," "I quit wanting anything because I couldn't get anything," "I am ugly," "I will fail my classes," "Everyone betrays me"), I advise the following:

- On a piece of paper similar to parchment paper, the consultant writes down all the self-criticisms from which she wishes to be free. She seals this list with a drop of blood and then buries it, planting above it a plant.

I had been working for twenty years on my first novel, *El loro de siete lenguas,* believing that it would never merit publishing. I wrote "failed writer" on a piece of parchment paper and buried it. Seven months later, I published the book, which was then followed by many others.

34. ABSENT FATHER (FOR A WOMAN)

In order to be loved when one reaches adulthood, it is absolutely necessary that the girl's incestuous drive acquires, as a goal, fusion with the father. In her unconscious, this will become her engine of desire. If the relationship with him is nonexistent (due to premature death, abandonment, or the mother's rejection), the adult woman feels an emptiness in her libido preventing her from establishing a stable relationship. In order to achieve the incestuous symbiosis, I recommend:

- The consultant should find a photograph of her father, roll it into a tube shape with the image facing outward, cover it with honey, and insert it into her vagina, keeping it there and remaining still, in bed, for three hours. Then she should remove it and climb to the top of the tallest building in the city and throw the tube as far as possible saying, "Now, dissolve yourself among the men!"

If the consultant cannot obtain a photo of the father—because the mother hated him and, wanting to forget him, did not save any photo—I advise:

- If the consultant knows his name, she should write it on a sugar cube and insert it into her vagina until it dissolves. (If the mother keeps secret the father's name, the word *dad* can be written on the sugar cube.)

35. ABSENT FATHER (FOR A MAN)

For the man to develop his adult virility, willpower, entrepreneurship, self-confidence, achievement capacity, guardian spirit, and kindheartedness, he will have to have been loved and brought up in childhood by a father with these characteristics. If the relationship was absent (due to premature death, absence, or rejection), the son, feeling an emptiness in his libido, will not be able to be independent and will establish relationships in which he acts subservient toward bosses, friends, and bossy women.

- So that the consultant's unconscious feels that he is supported by a parent, he should tattoo on the right arm his father's face and name. If the mother, out of hate, destroyed the photos of this absent one, or refuses to say his name, the consultant should tattoo in an indicated place a triangle with an eye inside it (the symbol of the eternal father).

  In any case, besides the tattoo, the consultant should put into the insoles of his shoes, until they rip, the four kings of a Tarot deck with the back facing down and the figures looking at the sole of the feet. In the right shoe, first place the King of Wands then the King of Spades on top. In the left foot, first place the King of Pentacles then the King of Cups on top. These four kings (symbols of the father) carry the sexual energy (Wands), the intellectual energy (Spades), the physical energy (Pentacles), and the emotional energy (Cups).

Apart from this, I advise the consultant to seek a teacher, of whatever subject—someone older who can give him free lessons in exchange for practical services.

36. EXPRESS REPRESSED RAGE

In the family's psychological climate, in which, from birth, the child was submerged, crazy ideas are mixed with unwanted feelings, frustrated desires, and actions guided by old concepts that do not correspond to current changes. This impresses upon the child that he should be what his parents or other relatives think he should be. If he does not obey these rules, he will be considered a traitor, sick, dumb, or "evil."

The family orders things the child does not want and denies the child what she wants. Family members prohibit her from being what she is, which leads her to be what others want her to be. The child, in this painful situation—and even though, to obtain love, she strives to be obedient—endures a repressed rage that is often buried in her unconscious. The child grows up believing that she was loved, that she has no problems. However, it may cost her the ability to establish a content family life. She fails in everything proposed, she complains of inexplicable depressions, or she suffers from a nervous disorder or develops manias. One day she realizes that she lives in constant suffering. It is the accumulated rage that doesn't allow her to enjoy life. I recommend the consultant do the following:

- Before anything, in order for the anger to grow up out of the depths of her unconscious, the consultant lies on her back on the floor and begins a tantrum, imitating a crisis of childish rage, slapping, kicking, allowing herself to bellow complaints and insults directed at whomever disappointed or harmed her.

The adult psyche tends to recycle its childish emotions. If due to a childish fear of ceasing to be loved the person does not dare to be aware of the errors of her relatives, professors, or friends, then, as an adult, she will project onto the coworkers or bosses who she believes love her that which the culprits projected onto her in the past. To be free, once the culprit(s) are identified, she can proceed to punish them in a metaphoric way in order to finally be relieved.

- A woman, recently divorced but still feeling furious toward her ex-husband, understanding that the ex is a projection of her militaristic and devastating father, taped a photograph of each man to a large watermelon that she destroyed with her kicks. She divided the pieces into two parts and sent half to the ex and placed the other half on her father's grave.

- If the pain was caused mostly by the mother (or an aunt, grandmother, sister), although this seems very cruel, the consultant should buy a black hen, beat it with a baseball bat until it is dead, then cook it and invite the one who is to blame to dinner, letting her eat the soup or stew of this beaten chicken. (If the aggressor has passed on, one should go to her grave site to kick it and urinate and defecate on it.)

- If it was an important person (father, boss), the consultant should go to his place of employment, his retirement home, or his grave and bomb it with a dozen raw eggs.

- To the consultant with suicidal wishes, who has suffered a long torment in a religious school, I recommend going in the early morning to the building and throwing an ostrich egg against the door. Reclaim the happiness in living.

- If it was a relative whom the consultant has already forgiven and whom, ultimately, in spite of everything the relative did, the consultant loves, I recommend going to the cemetery with a comb, water, and soap and cleaning the tombstone, then perfuming it, and finally, with a paintbrush dipped in honey, writing the word *love*.

Many times hate is a response to a never-obtained desire to be loved and recognized. However, to intellectually decide to forgive, because that is what the adults told us to do ever since we were children, inculcating in us a defective interpretation of the Gospels, is not healthy. These are the terms for a confrontation in order to forgive, whether it is with the person who has harmed us or with a therapist who represents the person or with a photograph or at the person's tombstone or, if the person was cremated, at the place where the ashes were scattered:

▶ 1. I have here what you did to me when I was a child.
2. This is what I felt back then.
3. This is what it caused in me.
4. This is what I continue feeling and suffering from to this day.
5. And this is the reparation I ask of you.

The consultant should evaluate the harm and demand a precise sum of money. I recommend that the consultant asks for millions. If the person, the actual person, rejects acknowledging the debt owed, the consultant must quit seeing the person until he has decided to fulfill the demand.

It serves nothing to ask, "I want you to hug me and to love me," "I want you to ask me for forgiveness," and so forth. What is the value of a damaged life? What does a failure neurosis cost? What is the value of a constant lack of self-esteem or frigidity, systematic self-destruction? For one of my kids, Cristóbal, I signed a huge metaphorical check for $3 million. He framed it and hung it in his consultation office.

▶ To definitively abandon the rage toward her parents, after a courageous confrontation, I recommend that the consultant burn a photograph of each of them. As an antidote, the consultant should take a pinch of the ashes of the father's burned photograph, dissolve this in a glass of wine, and drink it. Then take a pinch of the ashes of the mother's burned photograph, dissolve this in a glass of milk, and drink it.

37. DISTRESSING SECRETS

Every hidden secret turns into a pathological knot that slowly but surely invades the unconscious and, from this unimaginable zone, begins to exert a devastating action on the psyche (neurosis) and in the body (illnesses). With family, these secrets tend to surface, reproducing themselves through generations until someone confesses them. For example, if a grandmother conceals a rape, her daughter and granddaughter may also suffer from rape, repeating the trauma of this former act. The only way to end this distressing silence is to make a collection of energy by confessing the secret to as many relatives and friends as possible. It is probable that such a confession—that ends the clan's complicity, which prevents public disclosure of the secret and contradicts the facade of decency covering the secret, burying it in oblivion or ignoring it in spite of the message in the eyes of the members of the clan—will provoke disturbances in the consultant's life. But it is best to face expulsion from the clan rather than live as a prisoner of it, overwhelmed by prejudices and lack of understanding. The best way to reveal a secret is by a handwritten mailing.

▶ A consultant was married for twenty years to a premature ejaculator whose coitus did not last more than four seconds. He was not able to caress his wife but would abruptly open her legs to fulfill the brief rape. I recommended that she send a handwritten mailing to the whole family, describing her decision to ask her partner for a divorce and describing, in detail, the sexual acts that she had suffered for so many years. The family, for tradition and in defense of strict religious morals, favored the husband and called her crazy, a degenerate, a scoundrel and threatened to disinherit her. She did not give up, and she began a new and satisfactory life.

To homosexual and lesbian consultants, I recommend:

- If the families don't know, the consultant should communicate to them his or her sexual characteristics. To the consultants who object, "My father is homophobic, a perfect male chauvinist. If I tell him I am gay, he will kill me," I tell them: "He will not kill you, only his prejudices. But, I should tell you, after analyzing a multitude of genealogy trees, that children fulfill what the parents repress. It is very probable that your father has repressed his homosexual wishes. Intuitively, what you will confess to him, he already knows."

38. DOMINEERING PARENTS

Some domineering or possessive parents create failure neuroses in their children by making them feel guilty for getting away from them in order to live their own lives either out of the fear of being overtaken, enforced to advance what they were taught, or to draw on other sources. If they do not fulfill a united partnership through a true love, their children will feel guilty about uniting with a partner for love, or guilty for being successful when the parents were not successful. That is to say: the children are to become the parents themselves and go beyond that! In these cases, I advise:

- The consultant goes to visit the father and mother carrying, as a gift, a large bag full of chocolates in the shape of gold money. The consultant asks the parents to sit facing him, then the consultant tenderly pours the "money" like rain over the parents and presents them with a contract, saying, "With this money, I am paying you for all that you did for me, everything you gave me. If you love me, sign this contract."

  The following will be written in the contract: "Having been paid, we authorize our son [or daughter] to employ everything we taught him plus everything he learned on his own to pursue his talent in the world."

The consultant frames the contract and hangs it where he can see it every day.

39. THE INABILITY TO CARESS

For centuries, dark intentions have been attributed to touch. For example, a father may be afraid of his incestuous or homosexual impulses and caress his children with a love mixed with rejection due to a lack of self-confidence or because, undervaluing themselves, parents undervalue their children. Many children suffer psychological ills because their parents did not know how to caress them with due tenderness. And if the parents didn't caress, it was because they never knew an authentic tenderness from their own parents. In order to be able to caress someone well, awakening his or her essential nature, we should concentrate the physical, sexual, emotional, and mental strength into our hands, to feel in them infinite space and eternal time, the unmeasurable love that is the root of matter, the enormous happiness of life, and then touch that without suddenness, without overlapping sexual desires, without demonstration of power, but with devotion, concentrated attention, and mother-father goodness.

For the consultant who has not developed this necessary sensibility, I recommend:

- For a minimum of three months, the consultant caresses an inanimate object for half an hour each morning, trying to communicate life to it. This object can be a rock, a piano, a puppet or mannequin, a chair or other furniture, and so forth. Before doing this, the consultant should rub a piece of raw meat on his hands for seven minutes, which then is given to a cat or dog to eat, and wash the hands by soaping and rinsing them four times, one after the other, then cover them in a nice massage oil and perfume. At the end of some time thoroughly caressing the object, the consultant should notice how the object has absorbed the hands' heat, how the corners and the roughness have softened, and how the object seems to have acquired a soul. If the consultant is able to be sensitive like this to inanimate matter, he can caress a human being, revealing to the other the richness of tender physical contact.

40. TO STOP USING AGGRESSIVE LANGUAGE

Due to repressed disappointments and maybe for having been raised by parents who constantly criticized others in order to affirm their superiority, the consultant, in every phrase she speaks, slides in to aggressive words. This aggression, which for the most part is unconscious, is not only directed at whomever is around but also toward the society that shelters her and, ultimately, toward all of humanity. This is because the parents did not know how to recognize their daughter's values, and they destroyed the child's strengths in order to obtain minimum admiration. The nervous system's ultimate activity is to enunciate words, and these words are intimately linked to the body. Aggressive language, as if it were a boomerang, returns to whomever uses it and infects the mental and physical health, ending up forcing the speaker to cut friendly ties with kindred souls. I therefore recommend:

- The consultant gets some honeycomb and each morning, while otherwise fasting, sucks a piece of it. After sucking the honey and chewing the wax, she repeats three times, with the mouth sweetened: "Wherever there is no love, I will sew love, I will obtain love." The consultant keeps the rest of the comb in a gold container. When the consultant has collected a medium ball of masticated wax, she molds it into the shape of a heart, which, after submerging it in a crystal glass full of blessed water, she places in the center of the dining table or wherever she eats.

41. THE BLOCKED ARTIST

When an artist feels a constant inner call to fulfill an artistic work but, no matter how much the person wants to obey the call, cannot begin (possessed by an incomprehensible spiritual paralysis or by an anguished sloth), he may actually be complying with, in an unconscious way, a parental order; for example, parents who think that artists end up dying of hunger or that a woman who fulfills artistic goals will be in touch with unsavory people. If the consultant, in her childhood and adolescence, heard phrases like "All poets are fags," "All music is made by drug addicts," "All singers or actresses are sluts"; if the consultant belongs to a family that wishes him to adopt the father's "honorable and secure" profession; or if a woman is imprisoned in domestic work; and if we add to that parents who suppressed their own desires to be artists—which causes guilt for the offspring for doing what the parents could not do—then the consultant is stuck. So I recommend:

- If the consultant wants to write a book, he should pour a few drops of his urine into a jar of red ink and add a bit of saliva and a gram of excrement. With this, he handwrites the text's first three sentences or verses.

- If the consultant is lesbian, she should spread a spool of paper out, four feet long, on the floor, then take a bowl of black ink, spit in it seven times, and add to it a gram of excrement and a few drops of urine. She inserts the handle of a paintbrush into her vagina. She squats over the roll of paper with her legs open and knees bent, moving her hips, and advances sideways. In this manner, she will write the first five words of her text.

Both of the above manuscripts should be sent to the disapproving relatives. The same advice is valid for painters.

To a child, saliva, excrement, and urine—products made by one's body—are creative manifestations, but parents repress the pleasure the child has when playing with them.

42. AMENORRHEA

The human body (on a different plane than the psychic activity) can have animal behaviors. Sometimes, in the course of an analysis, the awareness of the cause of a disturbance through words is not effective. One must resort therefore to nonverbal actions that indicate to the body what is its healthy operation.

A laborer who worked for my father carrying merchandise in a donkey-drawn wagon could not fulfill his obligations because his stubborn donkey, not wanting to leave the corral, wouldn't move, refused to drink water, and dehydrated himself. He went to my father's shop to complain. "I don't know what to do. I try to force him to calm down, but he very stubbornly refuses." A gray-haired client, upon hearing this, told him, "It is a mistake to want to force the stubborn to do what they don't wish to do. I, too, have a donkey. Allow me to bring mine to you so that yours is not alone." With great curiosity, my father attended the meeting between the two animals and allowed me the pleasure of going along. The old man stood next to his donkey and placed a bucket full of water in front of him. The animal began to drink it up in huge gulps. The old man then put another bucket in front of the thirsty donkey, who immediately imitated his friend and began to drink.

Inspired by the events that I saw as a child, I suggest the following psychomagic act to a female consultant whose menstrual cycle has been disrupted. This act treats the organism of the consultant like the old man did with the stubborn donkey:

- The consultant buys a bottle of fake blood at a theater supply store and once every lunar month, for four days, imitates having a period by putting some of this blood into the vagina and preventing it from gushing out by using a tampon. After repeating this for four months, the consultant's period will return to normal.

43. AMOROUS JEALOUSY

Amorous jealousy is normal and expresses animalistic fear that a rival will take control of our partner. The more we fight intellectually against this instinctive feeling, accepting good reason to criticize the egoism and advocate for trust and generosity, the less possible it is to convince the person's emotional and sexual centers to quit worrying when the partner travels or is absent longer than normal. Instead of trying to eliminate the jealousy, I advise the jealous consultant to make positive use of the jealousy:

- The consultant finds a beautiful, transparent bottle into which, each time she feels jealous, she deposits a $1 bill (if she is not financially stable), a $20 bill (if her financial position is a bit more secure), or a $100 bill (if she has financial stability). When the money has accumulated, the consultant buys a gift for her lover.

44. INSANE JEALOUSY

When the consultant's jealousy reaches delirium and she wants to be free of this agonizing madness that forces her to think her partner wants to seduce the whole world and only wants to trick the consultant, it means that the consultant is the one who projects her repressed, homosexual desires onto the companion. Following the maxim of François de La Rochefoucauld (1613–1680), "Jealousy nourishes doubt and makes it rabid or it is extinguished as it passes from doubt to certainty." I advise:

- To the jealous man: with a photograph of his own face, he should make a mask for his partner. Then the consultant must observe four nude men, recruited from the porn industry, caress his also nude partner. In this way, seeing his face on his partner's body, he will fulfill his drives and the jealousy will end. To the jealous woman: in this case, the recruited sex workers will be women and her partner will wear a mask made with a photograph of herself.

45. FAILURE NEUROSIS

If the consultant undertakes a task but never finishes it; if every time the consultant succeeds in something, he manages to turn this victory into a failure; if each time the consultant manages to form a pleasurable partnership with someone, she ends up causing conflicts, which end in separation; if the consultant is harassed by an incomprehensible guilt; if the consultant constantly feels dissatisfied with himself; if, in spite of having talent and in spite of all efforts, he does not succeed—the consultant suffers with a failure neurosis. This is due to one (or all) of six main causes. When a consultant complains of never completing what she starts or if she is distressed to think of achieving success, I ask her which of these six main causes of the failure neurosis has she endured: it can be one, several, or all. For each cause, I suggest an act.

1. Having been a burden on the family

The child may have been born at a moment of financial difficulty for the parents; the child may have been begotten by accident; the child may have been born into a very large family; the child's birth may have forced the mother to sacrifice her fulfillment; the child's parents may have felt themselves forced into marriage—and so forth.

▶ The consultant, to be free of this depressing feeling, should get a big suitcase with wheels and fill it with bones and meat for dogs bought from the butcher. The suitcase's load should weigh as much as the consultant's body. This done, the consultant should drag it for three miles down a street toward a river or ocean in the consultant's birth city, where the consultant should throw the suitcase into the water (in the absence of a body of water, the consultant should bury it). If the consultant lives very far away, and it is impossible to travel there, the consultant may do this in a city whose name begins with the same first letter as the consultant's birth city, for example, Toledo (Spain) can represent Toulouse (France) or Tijuana (Mexico) or Tempe (Arizona).

After doing this, the consultant should invite his parents to a balloon ride. During this trip, the consultant should give them hugs and, without explanation, give them a bag full of chocolates in the shape of gold coins. If the parents are dead or divorced or if they refuse to make the trip, the consultant should make the trip in the company of two friends or therapists (a man and a woman): the male will wear a mask of the consultant's father; the woman, the consultant's mother.

2. Not being what the parents wanted you to be

They wanted a boy and you were a girl, or vice versa. The mother wanted you to look like her, and you came out looking like your father, or the opposite. They hoped for a silent offspring, and you came out screaming: "You cried so much that, exhausted by lack of sleep, we wanted to kill you." They thought you were ugly: "No one is going to want to marry you." You were willful: "You were a very bad child." You were obese: "We were following a spiritual path, and the only thing you wanted to do was eat."

► If the parents made known their dissatisfaction with the consultant for having been born a woman (when they hoped for a boy) and due to this attitude a lack of self-esteem was produced, I advise the consultant to visit her parents dressed as a man and to cut a few of her hairs into very small pieces and glue them onto her face to mimic stubble. Like this, she should say to them, "This is the way you wanted to see me: a man without a penis, incomplete. But, I am not this." Then the consultant should take off her clothes and, showing her naked self to them, say, "Now is the time to see me just as I am: a complete woman. Take me in your arms and ask me to forgive you. If you don't, you will never see me again."

- If the parents made it known their dissatisfaction with the consultant for having been born a man (when they hoped for a girl), I advise the consultant to visit his parents dressed as a woman and ask them for money to buy a plane ticket to go to Brazil because he wants to amputate his penis to change his gender. When he sees them dismayed, he should laugh, telling them that it is a joke though it is necessary so that they realize that this is what they wished for all of his life. He should then disrobe and violently throw the woman's clothes at their faces while screaming, "Stop! Look at me! I have testicles! I have a cock! I am a man!"

- To the consultant whose parents told her, "You are ugly," I recommend that she make a mask with the photograph of the face of a movie star who is considered beautiful. With the mask on, the consultant should sit on a bench in a public place and remain still with a sign hung from her neck with this message (written in capital letters), "I am beautiful, but I have an ugly soul." The following day, the consultant should return to the same place but with a mask made with a photograph of her face, made up as ugly as possible, and with a sign that reads, "I am ugly, but I have a beautiful soul." On the third day, the consultant should return with a mask made with a photograph of her face exactly as it is and a sign that reads, "Quit judging me. I am neither beautiful or ugly. I am what I am. Who wants to meet me?" The consultant should converse with the people who draw near, removing the mask.

To eliminate the feeling of not being what one should be, if the consultant does not have the presence or collaboration of her parents, I advise:

- The consultant makes a garment like those used by members of the Ku Klux Klan, with a tunic and a hood to hide her head, but red not white. Dressed like that, the consultant walks through different, very populated city places and, if it is possible, visits relatives and friends, while acting and conversing with them as if the consultant doesn't realize she is dressed up. At night, the consultant must remove the disguise, fold it up very carefully, and urinate on it, then pack it into a gift box and send it, anonymously, to her parents.

3. Having betrayed the family beliefs

From generation to generation, from distant ancestors, ideas and beliefs are transmitted, which the majority of the time, unconsciously, constitute the commandments that maintain family coherence. These roots are always from religious origins. Even in atheist clans, morals are descended from holy books hidden in the shadows. So that the clan survives, it asks the child to commune with the family's guiding principles. Then, when the child grows up, if he changes the ideas and beliefs (instilled in him by others) for ideas and beliefs that better suit him now, the family disowns him. This, in an unconscious way, causes a guilt that drives the consultant to punish himself by failure.

- The consultant must put in a backpack the Bible (Old and New Testaments), the Koran, *Das Kapital* by Karl Marx, and *Mein Kampf* by Adolf Hitler. He carries this backpack with the five books in it for three days (only taking the backpack off to sleep or to bathe). Then the consultant buries these books in a large planter over which he plants a bonsai, or a miniature tree. The consultant should let the tree grow freely, after having already pruned it. (Some professionals, in order to sell them later, shape the young sprouts of a planted branch with wire, which gives the buyer, who will be continuously pruning the new shoots, a way to mimic "creating" a dwarf tree.)

4. Having departed from or having been cut off from the family

A healthy family agrees to form part of a collective, the same way that a tree is part of the forest. This family refuses to define a whole by one of its different parts: the world is not negative. Each member of the family acknowledges that there is a lot of negativity within him- or herself, but each member collaborates with the others to eradicate this negativity and also to accept the arrival of new members who bring other customs, ideas, and beliefs. On the other hand, members of a neurotic, incestuous, and narcissistic family consider themselves at war with others: the world is negative and one must protect oneself from it. The home is converted into a refuge or fortress. To go away from the family is to deprive it of its defense. The clan sees this as a loss of strength: "We gave you our energy, our time. Now that you are leaving, what is going to happen to us?" "We gave you life so that you would take care of us later." "Your great-grandfather founded our business, your grandfather inherited it, and then I did: your father. You must continue it. You can't just go live your life!"

▶ To remove the guilt hidden in the consultant's unconscious over having left the family home (left the clan), the consultant must convince the unconscious to allow freedom. For this, the consultant will stage this symbolic act: tie one end of a two-foot-long chain to her waist and attach the other end of the chain to two empty tin cans: one with a photograph of the consultant's father fastened to it, the other with a photograph of the consultant's mother. The consultant carries a saw to cut metal in her hands while dragging the chain on the ground with the cans. Making no attempt to muffle the noise the cans make, the consultant drags them for three miles along a busy road toward the office of a Freudian psychoanalyst with whom the consultant has a prearranged appointment. Face-to-face with the therapist, the consultant asks him to cut the chain with the saw.

Having performed this act, the consultant buries the chain and plants a fruit tree over it. Then she fills the two cans with the photographs with acacia honey, puts them in a waterproof box, and throws the box into the river for the current to take away. If there is no river in the consultant's city, she should travel to a city with a river.

5. Achieving what one's parents wanted but could not get

In each generation, the new members of the family are forced to be not what they are (individuals who develop their awareness by obeying the motions of the future) but to be what the clan wants them to be (individuals who obey the limitations imposed on them by the past and who sacrifice their dreams). Parents who were similarly repressed cause their children painful conflicts: "We want you to be fulfilled and to have what we could not have but, if you do this, you will destroy us by undermining the clan's principles. We loved you because you are like us. If you are different, we will stop loving you." Some years ago, a movie called *Shine* premiered in which a talented pianist, the son of a failed pianist, managed to succeed. Upon achieving this success and feeling guilty about it, he went crazy.

▶ The consultant should visit, with a gold-painted face, his parents, bringing them each an expensive wristwatch along with twenty fake gold bricks made of plaster and a contract handwritten on parchment paper. Standing before them, the consultant takes them by the hand and, very respectfully, says, "Mom and Dad, I give you these watches to express the love I have had for you all my life. I have also brought you each ten gold bricks to pay for everything you have given me. And now I want you to sign this contract, which states: 'Our child can now use everything we have taught him because he has paid for it in gold and in love. Having thus paid, our child can now use it all to enrich and enhance himself through more training and/or experiences. Signed with our blood: Your Parents.'"

The consultant should promptly offer them a red ink fountain pen with which to sign the contract. If they are divorced or dead, the consultant may fulfill this act with two friends (a man and a woman) or two therapists.

6. Repressed juvenile sexuality

Some old-fashioned, conservative parents consider sexual pleasure to be a sin, and they punish their children whenever they show sexual curiosity or play with their body parts, which religious education classifies as "private." A mother harshly scolds a very small girl for touching her father's penis when he gets up naked in the morning. In another case, the parents force a little boy to wear boxing gloves when he goes to bed out of fear that he will masturbate. A mother, seeing her son touch his penis, slaps his hand and, in disgust, says, "Pig!" These episodes cause these little ones to feel guilty about their sexual pleasure, which later extends to their feeling guilty about any pleasure whatsoever, including, among other things, the pleasure of having succeeded in any task undertaken.

▶ The consultant should go to a sex shop, dressed as a five-year-old boy (or girl) and in the company of two therapists (a man and a woman). The man should wear a necklace with a framed photograph of the consultant's father hanging from it. The woman should do the same with a framed photograph of the mother. All three should shut themselves into a booth and, for three hours, watch pornographic films chosen by the "child," obeying his curiosity. After this long projection, while watching the last film, the consultant should, leaving aside all modesty, masturbate in front of the two therapists, who hug the consultant and kiss his cheek when he reaches orgasm. The therapists should say to the consultant, "You are a good kid." Then, remaining in their costumes, the three will go to a tearoom for desserts. The next day, the consultant will either send the child's costume to his parents or split it in two and leave it at their graves.

46. GATHER STRENGTH BEFORE A RADICAL CHANGE

One can define life in two words: permanent impermanence. The world economic crises, troubles at work, with the family, in relationships, the unexpected successes, and so forth constantly provoke changes in our lives. At times these changes are radical, and we do not feel prepared to take them on. We fear that others will notice our insecurities. How, then, do we conceal these at the same time as we gather strength? To those who suffer from such a situation, I advise:

- The consultant plasters her leg and goes wherever is required, with the limp and with crutches, telling the story of how, in a terrible accident, she broke her leg. At the end of a reasonable amount of time, the consultant removes the cast but continues to simulate the limp: returning to her normal walk little by little. In this moment, the consultant will be completely accustomed to her new situation.

47. INABILITY TO CONCENTRATE

When someone is unable to concentrate because he is always afflicted by multiple interests, and he jumps from one idea to another or from one feeling to another, he is saying that in his infancy he lacked parents who gave him necessary attention. When we become adults, we continue treating ourselves the way our parents treated us, not giving to ourselves what we were not given during childhood. In this case, the consultant, repeating the childhood situation, does not give himself necessary attention and, therefore, denies the being. I therefore advise:

- The consultant should go plant a tree as close as possible to her birthplace. Then she should take home ten pounds of soil from this region and pour it out onto a plastic sheet. The consultant should kneel over this soil and submerge her head in a container full of water, holding her breath until she feels like she is going to drown. She pulls out her head when she is overwhelmed by mortal angst. The consultant will repeat this operation, successively, seven times. Such an act will be repeated every morning while fasting for eighteen days. The birth soil will be deposited in a pot, and a cactus in the shape of an elongated spine will be planted there.

48. STOLEN CHILDHOOD

Some toxic, immature parents behave like children of their children, making these children (from a very early age) partners in their problems. The children advise and encourage this kind of parent. Behaving in this childish way, these parents turn their children into adults before their time. The heavy responsibility that the parents toss on top of the children prevents the children from developing the most important activity for a child: to play. Because of this, these children grow up repressing a continuous sadness; they do not know how to entertain themselves. The only thing they know is how to acquire responsibility, helping others but forgetting themselves. I therefore advise the consultant to:

- The consultant gathers together a respectable sum of money and goes to a casino, changes the money into the lowest sum token, and plays until all the money is lost. The consultant does not gamble to win; he gambles to lose (losing requires more play!). Even if the consultant wins and accumulates a fortune, he must play until all of the money is gone. In this way, the consultant will discover the joy of acting without a utilitarian purpose.

49. FAMILY ILLNESSES

Many people who suffer from illnesses that have been repeated for generations think these illnesses are congenital. They say, for example, "We Gauleys were born with weak livers" or "In our family, everyone suffers from heart disease." The grandmother dies of breast cancer as do the mother and the granddaughter. The father belches constantly and has polyps in his nose, and the son also has these troubles. If a great-grandfather returned from the trenches of the war of 1914 with lungs gnawed by gases, many of his descendants suffer from lung diseases.

Families, set up like clans, have common bonds and interests to protect them. To belong to a tribe is to have the security to be loved, and you will not want or need for anything. If a member commits an act that undermines the clan's unity, that member will be punished by expulsion. The primitive belief that the excluded one cannot survive in the middle of aggressive nature is maintained in the deep unconscious. Expulsion is felt as a death sentence. The oldest punishment issued by the church is excommunication. This unconscious drive to not be excluded from the community (in families where amorous expression is not manifested clearly) is expressed through "common disease," which clearly indicates group membership. The brain, to avoid suffering, will always choose the lesser of two evils. This causes the individual to prefer to suffer from a sometimes deadly illness, which identifies him or her as a member of the family, rather than live in ancestral terror of being abandoned. Therefore, I recommend:

- The consultant chooses any object to represent his illness (a heavy book, a family photo album, a stone, a dissected animal), puts it in a bag, and, for forty days, takes it with him every time he leaves the house. At the end of this period, the consultant goes to the tomb of his oldest ancestor and leaves the object there, pouring little vials of honey over it while saying these words, "Dearest ancestor, I do not need your illness in order to be united with the tribe." Then the consultant sends, by post, to every member of the family, a vial of honey similar to the one used to pour honey over the object representing the family illness.

50. RIDDING OURSELVES OF LABELS

Although often with good intentions, our parents and teachers attribute negative definitions to us, which last for many years and prevent us from developing ourselves with pleasure. In psychomagic, we call these definitions "labels" because they stick to the self. So that the consultant can free herself from them, I advise:

- The consultant writes on adhesive labels as many definitions as they gave her, for example: "You have no ear for music," "You don't know how to use your hands," "You're a freeloader, liar, thief," "You're egotistical, weak, dumb, fat, skinny, vain, ungrateful," and so on. The consultant glues these labels to every part of the body—many of them to the face—and goes out in public that way for as many hours as possible. When the consultant returns home, she should remove the labels, roll them into a ball, take the ball to the city dump, and throw it on top of the garbage pile, having beforehand caressed her body with hands soaked in pleasant perfume.

51. DIFFICULTY CARRYING PREGNANCY TO TERM

Many women suffer from, in spite of having no physical defect, an inability to become mothers. Analyzing their genealogy trees, one understands that, unconsciously, these women do not really want to be mothers, they are afraid, or it is forbidden. Some ancestors sacrificed their lives raising lots of offspring or they died giving birth or their experience was terribly painful or they married men they hated or they delivered their babies and were widowed at about the same time. This anguish over being a mother is transmitted from one generation to the next until it is rooted in the unconscious. Furthermore, if the woman's mother caused her to suffer, the woman will want to be anything but a mother: during delivery she will feel like she has turned into her perpetrator. As if by chance, these women will form partnerships with men who, due to hating the characters of their fathers and not wanting to become their fathers, will also experience difficulty with fertility. In some cases, this is combined with parents who wanted a boy but, instead, raised their daughter as an unsuccessful boy. This causes anguish during pregnancy for fear of losing parental love, disappointing them. Last, as the firstborn, a person has seen that the birth of a little brother or sister robs the parents' attention from the older sibling. Jealousy makes the sibling hate the mother's "traitor" pregnancy, thus she swears, unconsciously, to never get pregnant. One can also follow another track: when the consultant was young she repressed and blamed herself for her incestuous impulses toward her father due to her innocent desire to make a child with her father—imitating her mother. As an adult, the blaming continues to act such that the shadow of her desire to be a mother is threatened by the incest impulse toward her own father.

I recommend, after looking at all of the incentives for the sterility, the consultant must stop asking herself what within her is the culprit—the rational way—and perform a ceremony to include all the possibilities, allowing her unconscious to choose its healing path.

- Using a large pillow, the consultant pretends to be nine-months pregnant and also dresses provocatively, like a prostitute. She wears a bridal headdress and carries a doll in her arms. Her husband or lover will accompany her wearing a photograph of the consultant's father's face. The consultant will seek permission from her friends to allow their kids (no matter what age) to accompany her. Surrounded by children, they will take a walk around a busy area and stop to have ice cream and pastries at a café. The man accompanying the pretend pregnant woman will feed her the ice cream and pastry. The parents of the children—who have followed at a discreet distance—will give ice cream and pastries to the children. The couple will take a taxi and, while the car is in motion, taking them home, will throw passport-sized photocopies of photographs of the consultant's mother's face and the father's face of the consultant's partner. Each will throw one hundred and fifty photocopies out. The following day, in a gift box, the consultant will send her father the bride's veil and the doll. Then she and her partner will bury the prostitute costume and the fake belly, planting a fruit tree above the grave.

In families where there is a tradition of single women, the consultant (due to desires to belong to the clan) can grow up fearing but unconsciously desiring to remain single. When she marries, she lives in anguish of being abandoned, feeling incapable of bearing children. These women live out their genealogy trees like a curse. Following is what I recommend in order to heal:

- I propose that the consultant finds a woman who has been married for more than twenty years, and the woman blesses her (putting the woman's hand to the consultant's forehead). The consultant should repeat this with nineteen other women who have been married for more than twenty years. If the consultant manages to succeed, it is possible that she will have children and remain in a partnership for more than twenty years.

If the consultant no longer has her ovaries yet persistently suffers with the desire to be a mother, I recommend the following:

- The consultant finds a fertilized chicken egg and inserts it into her vagina until the chick hatches. (Guy de Maupassant, the writer, wrote a story about a woman, lying paralyzed in her bed, whose husband surrounded her with eggs. Seeing the eggs hatch after incubating from her body heat, the woman regained her self-esteem.)

I received this card from Valencia, Spain:

> I went to Paris for you to read my Tarot. I commented that I was having problems staying pregnant. You gave me a psychomagic act. . . . [W]ith a mask made with a photograph of the face of my mother, I made love with my partner while he looked at me through a handheld mirror. With his ejaculation, I removed the mask and looked at myself in the mirror. Three months after the act, I was pregnant.

52. NO PARTNER

In the magic and witchcraft treatments, the majority of the recipes are destined to charm a person into loving us. An ancient, anonymous treaty, *Livre de secrets de la Magie,* stored at the Bibliothèque de l'Arsenal in Paris, offers this medieval recipe:

- The consultant obtains some physical element of the person who she wants to bewitch (saliva, blood, hair, finger, or toenails) or whatever object is imbued with the person: a piece of clothing, and so forth. She wraps the object up in a red ribbon on which the consultant has written in her blood both names. The consultant folds the ribbon so the names touch. She encloses this charm in the mounted body of a sparrow for seven days. Then the consultant carries it under her armpit for another seven days. Afterward the consultant throws it into the fire. As the charm burns, the consultant goes to visit the person she loves and finds that person bewitched and ready to submit to the consultant.

What I want to say is that if we need to fulfill such a complicated hex it is because the desired one rejects us or is an impossible ideal. All amorous obsession for a person who will never satisfy our desires is the creeping of incestuous, infantile drives aimed at our mother or father. We want this object of our obsession to be devoted to us, yet we do everything to ensure that it doesn't happen.

The majority of single people who complain about not having opportunities to find a partner are ultimately, due to different traumas and conflicts, warding off this union. To find someone, the consultant must stop preventing it and make himself available, not toward a being he determines he wants but toward whomever the universal forces desire to unite him with. It is necessary then to convince the unconscious to help the consultant. One can do this by following two paths: one slow and the other fast. The slow path requires an analysis of the genealogy tree and a courageous consultant who is not afraid to confront painful memories in order to free herself from the incest trap. The fast path is the path of psychomagic, which only requires faith.

- I advise the male consultant to tie to his penis a pink ribbon upon which he has written in green ink: "I need a woman." The female consultant should tie a light blue ribbon around her waist upon which she has written in red ink: "I need a man."

The consultant (male or female) should recite, screaming: "Let him [or her] come! And let no one detain him [or her]!" Without detaching the ribbon, this is to be carried out at six in the morning, six in the evening, and at midnight for three days in a row while the consultant looks intently at him- or herself in a mirror.

The Mexican medicine woman Pachita—a subtle expert of the human soul—recommended this spell, which may very well make up bits of my psychomagic recipes.

▶ Darling son, take a piece of amber—and if it is possible a piece with an insect embedded in its interior—and hold it in your closed, left hand. Put this hand over your heart, close your eyes, and concentrate on the kind of person you want to attract. Imagine her with all of the details you can: height, weight, eye and hair color, life interests, activities that you would like her to do. Imagine yourself with this person, lying together in bed.

Now kiss the amber and place it in a pink handkerchief made of silk, then wrap it up securely. Take it with you every day for seven days wherever you go, and sleep with this amber under your pillow. Repeat everything daily—visualize while holding the amber in your hand but don't uncover it. Around the seventh day, you will find someone very similar to the person in your vision.

The consultant, seeing an unknown person, finds love at first sight and fervently wants to form a partnership with this person because the consultant believes this person is the right woman or man, but the consultant nevertheless doesn't feel capable of conquering this person. This means that the overlapping Oedipal drives are forcing the consultant to want an impossible love, and the unconscious will ensure that the consultant's romantic dream is unfulfilled, forcing the consultant to act so awkwardly that he or she will be rejected. So that this does not occur, the consultant should make the unconscious instill total confidence and ensure success by way of the following ancient magic recipe:

- The consultant places a lamb's heart on a wooden table and a photograph or drawing of the desired person atop this heart. He molds a phallus from rose petals (if the consultant is a woman, an oval) to encircle the lamb's heart and picture. With a needle, he pricks the right ring finger and lets seven drops of blood fall over the picture. With the same needle, he pierces the picture and the heart while repeating one hundred times the person's name. Once the consultant has done this, at midnight, he burns all of the elements in a blazing outdoor bonfire.

53. WARTS

Warts are a problem aligned with the sufferer's psychological state. A Chilean psychologist who worked in Paris came to consult with me because a big wart had grown on the sole of his left foot, which made it difficult to walk. His doctor told him it was necessary to apply acid on it for more than a year to eliminate it. The consultant explained that some studies on the symbolism of the human body related the left foot with the mother and the right foot with the father. He confessed to me that his mother raised him alone, his father having abandoned her, and this established a solid bond between him and his mother.

"How long has it been since you visited your mother?"

"Four years!"

"Maybe this wart, making you aware of your steps, is produced by a feeling of guilt: 'You abandoned me just like your father did.' You should go see her."

"I deeply want to but it is impossible. I have unavoidable work commitments."

I proposed the following to the psychologist:

- Make several copies of a photograph of your mother. With these photocopies, make insoles and put one in the left shoe with your mother's face facing the sole of the bare foot. You should keep it there until wear begins to erase her image, then change it for another one.

The consultant did this and the wart disappeared at the end of two weeks.

For consultants with any other type of psychological problem, I advise:

- The consultant should rub the warts with a piece of raw steak, then toss it to a dog passing in the street: for the unconscious, the dog is a guard animal. Upon committing this act, the consultant should whisper, "Carry this far from me."

The grandmother of the French cartoonist François Boucq cured warts by rubbing them with an onion once a day for nine days. She then buried the onion, and when the onion had rotted, the warts had disappeared. Somehow this common-sense recipe and my advice use similar techniques: rubbing the wart with an organic element (raw meat or onion), which absorbs the essence of the wart. Even if one does not believe in such things, one may accept that it gives, for the unconscious, reality to all symbolic acts, and this is certain. The organic element, loaded in this way, transfers it to the animal who eats the meat and, thereby, destroys the wart, or to the earth, which devours it.

The rubbing should not be defensive or aggressive but delicate and friendly as if they were caresses. The unconscious sends us illnesses as if they were messengers so that, escaping the moral barrier that prevents our basic instincts to become present, they transfer valuable information to our rational side. Rather than fight an illness, seeing it as a fatal enemy, it is better to imagine it as a respectable entity and to adopt it and seduce it, thanking it for compelling us to take care of our bodies and freeing us in this way from the delusions in which we hide in order to not confront boldly our traumas and conflicts.

54. KLEPTOMANIA

When a person who steals (not for material necessity but for irresistible impulses) decides to confess her vice to a relative or therapist, she has taken the first step toward healing. This problem is born from some childhood trauma. Upon the birth of a little brother or sister, a child who demonstrates disgust over feeling deprived of maternal care and is therefore severely punished (for this natural jealousy) may then want to confiscate someone else's objects: fueled by a desire to rob his opponent's affection. I therefore recommend the following:

- The consultant gets her hands dirty in mud and asks her parents (or, in their absence, two friendly people: a man and a woman) to wash them off several times with soap, rinsing them with holy water and perfuming them. Then the consultant, carrying several handwritten cards in her pocket, visits a big store (or whatever business appeals to the consultant), and having chosen the object that she wants to steal, she places one of the cards next to the object without drawing any attention to the act. The cards should read: "I am _______ [with the consultant's name written in diminutive: Johnny, Kathy], the child thief. I could have stolen this, but I didn't. I have succeeded! Love me."

55. GUILT ATTACKS

Sometimes, for no apparent reason, people feel guilty without knowing why. With all certainty this must be repressed childhood urges. Not everyone is willing to thoroughly follow the deep advice engraved on the Temple of Apollo at Delphi in ancient Greece: "Know thyself." There are many things we prefer to keep in the darkness of the unconscious. We feel that we do not have problems and that we do not want to complicate our lives by opening old wounds to remove inconsolable pain. In order to conveniently be rid of irrational guilt attacks, I propose, first of all:

► The consultant goes to a spa or a health resort to take a mud bath and lets his bad mood out while growling, "I am not guilty of anything. A dirtiness that does not belong to me is polluting my soul. Stop! I am going to clean myself: first me and then my whole genealogy tree." Once cleaned, dried, perfumed, and dressed in new clothes, the consultant should return to his house and stand in front of a floodlight to project his shadow on a plastic sheet spread out on the floor. A beloved or intimate friend (or in his or her absence, a therapist) should carefully wash with water, soap, and a brush the consultant's shadow then dry and perfume it, while the consultant remains completely still. The plastic sheet should be put into a black bag to reuse, in case another attack of guilt ensues.

Already feeling better, the consultant should go to a cemetery carrying a receptacle full of water, soap, a scrub brush, and spray perfume. The consultant should then clean and perfume fourteen tombstones: for seven men and seven women. In front of each, the consultant should say a different word: father, mother, paternal grandmother, paternal grandfather, maternal grandmother, maternal grandfather, great-grandmother (four times), and great-grandfather (another four times).

Sometimes, without meaning to, we make mistakes that we see as moral debts and we feel ourselves incapable of fixing the harm we have done. In this case, I recommend that the consultant, first of all, acknowledge the debt then appraise it and pay it.

An Algerian woman suffered endless guilt over laughing, instead of crying, when she witnessed from afar the explosion that killed her parents. I recommended that she invest as much money as possible to buy jewelry, to then travel (while wearing these treasures) to the city where her parents died, and to bury the jewelry as close as possible to the place where the explosion took place.

56. MALE COWARDICE

In general, cowardice has its origin in a severe father who punished and terrorized the child, threatening to crush him, as his method for raising a child. However, the greatest terror we can experience in childhood (together with the greatest love) comes from a mother. Being the fountain of one's life, she is presented to us as an all-powerful goddess who, at any moment, can end our lives. The scared man feels embarrassed, a "little man" who is unconsciously longing to be stronger than his father in order to defeat the mother dragon. I advise the following:

- For one year, once every twenty-eight days (a lunar month), the consultant goes to a supermarket and steals a beefsteak. He hides it in his underpants and wraps his testicles with it (in order to absorb the power of this female flesh). At home, the consultant should grill it, eat half of it, and give the other half to a male animal (cat or dog).

  In order not to accumulate guilt, after each robbery, the consultant should send an anonymous card to the supermarket's manager enclosing the exact sum of the cost of the beefsteak.

57. IMPOTENCY

Some men who have problems with erections when they sleep with women are suppressing a childish rage against their mothers who didn't pamper them at the appropriate moment. These men want to punish their mothers. This suppressed hatred (which, articulated, would awaken the terror of being castrated by his mother) is turned on any woman who shows an interest in having sexual relations with them. The desire to cruelly avenge the childhood disappointment of not being loved inhibits a man's libido, leading to impotency. To achieve his erection, I recommend an act to the consultant in order to allow him to metaphorically fulfill his sadism.

▶ The consultant must obtain a horsewhip, a hard cushion, a jar full of fake blood (or, in its absence, red paint), and a brush, two-inches wide. His lover, a generous accomplice, inserts a rolled-up photograph of the consultant's mother into her vagina and places herself on her knees in front of him with her back to him and her hands on the floor to support her. To the side of her is the cushion. Screaming in rage, the consultant, with the right hand, lays a ferocious lash on the cushion. With the left hand holding the brush dipped in the fake blood (or paint), the consultant traces a long red line on the woman's back, and he continues to act out his anger with lashes and strokes until the female body is covered in red lines. Then, standing up, he goes to one corner in the room. On all fours, she goes to the opposite corner. Vulgarly and threatening her with the whip, he screams, "Come suck my dick, bitch!" She advances with her tongue out, like an animal, and he continues with the insults until fellatio is complete.

58. STUTTERING

Stuttering is caused from the lack of a conscious father to provide the child with true affection and the moral and spiritual training the child needs. A childish, narcissistic, or tyrannical father creates, in the child, an accumulation of suppressed energy due to the child's inability to be herself, as she is required to submit to the paternal inaptitude. This submission will affect her self-esteem in adulthood, with her feeling diminished by her stuttering and a prisoner of an endless childhood. I recommend the following:

- The consultant finds a heterosexual man (a teacher, a guru, a therapist) old enough to be his father and who has begotten children. The consultant asks the elder to stand in front of him, face him, take his testicles and penis, and, with deep energy, transmit his virile power there. While this takes place, the consultant recites a poem aloud (any poem he chooses).

I received this e-mail:

> I am studying speech therapy, and my thesis relates to psychomagic and the work of a speech therapist, mainly basing my thesis on addressing the individual in all of his/her bio-psychosocial complexity. At any rate, I do not see how to convince a speech therapist of the power that the metaphor and its symbolism can have. I heard you have cured a large number of stutterers (all men). Could you apply this psychomagic to a female stutterer, someone with autism, or a mute child?

I responded with the following acts:

- A female stutterer has not approached me, but I believe I would hug her with all my might and press my heart against hers until our heartbeats become one rhythm. Then she should recite a poem by shouting.

- I have been in contact with an autistic person who, seated and immobile, always looks at the floor. I got on my back and put myself in the area of his look. Upon seeing me in his world, he communicated with me.

- A woman, in an autistic crisis, was naked in her bathtub. Without undressing or taking off my shoes, I got into the water with her and sat in front of her and successfully communicated with her.

- I asked a mother to rub honey—acacia or chestnut, because they are liquid—all over her mute child and then completely lick the honey off the child's body while whispering a lullaby.

The metaphors and symbols should materialize into actions.

59. MORNING SLUGGISHNESS

There is a popular saying that goes, "Laziness is the mother of all vices." A saying that can be reduced to, "Laziness is mother." If the consultant is incapable of getting up early in the morning, robbing time from the beginning of the day, the consultant is a prisoner of childish indiscipline and longs for a loving mother. To begin one's day means to grow, to become an adult. The bed is a substitute for the maternal womb that never ends the gestation. As the lack of discipline will not allow the consultant to undergo psychoanalysis, I recommend a purely practical act:

- Before going to bed, the consultant should drink two liters of water. The need to urinate will awaken the consultant early and force him out of bed. If laziness still persists, the consultant should simply give himself permission to urinate in the bed. The discomfort this will cause will convince the consultant to get out of bed the following morning to drain himself.

60. RECOVERING FAITH IN ONESELF

Some consultants feel hopeless and think all of their decisions have been mistakes. The feeling of being unable to trust one's own judgment terrifies them. To these consultants, I recommend:

- Each morning for one month, the consultant should go out for a walk wearing spectacles that have metal circles in place of glass lenses. Blinded in this way, guided only by a white stick, the consultant walks around the block three times.

61. INTELLECTUAL ANXIETY

A consultant may feel imprisoned in her mind. She believes all words are lies and considers them useless for expressing feelings. I recommend:

- The consultant should shave her head in front of a mirror, then, on this naked cranium, paint in red nail polish the word *no*.

A Spanish consultant wrote to me for help to "get out of my head." I responded:

- Go to FNAC [a four-story megastore of media fare] in Madrid wearing an overcoat but naked underneath. (On the third floor, a friend will be waiting for you with another overcoat.) On the first floor, quickly hurl your coat off and ride the escalator up while screaming, "I am an intellectual learning to die!" On the third floor, cover yourself with the overcoat awaiting you, and give the friend a kiss with the tongue. (If you are homosexual, the friend should be male or, in the absence of a male friend for this act, then it should be a woman who is over seventy years old.)

62. SEXUAL ABUSE

When a father abuses a daughter, he often doesn't do it in a violent way, but he does so through seduction thereby making her an accomplice. The little girl doesn't resist because she feels that this is the way in which her father demonstrates his affection, and she can demonstrate hers. This produces a sexual bond, terrible suffering, and deep guilt. As an adult, in the sexual and emotional facets, the daughter sees herself subject to the desires of men, and while her partner(s) may see her as a great lover, she can count her orgasms on one hand. She fakes and adjusts her pleasure to her partner's desires to, above all, guarantee that he won't abandon her, which reproduces the childhood situation when the little girl was an object of pleasure even though she was not prepared to feel something for someone. In the economic aspect, her uncertain and unstable life imitates her childhood dependence. To sum it up, even though the years pass, she continues to be possessed by her father. (Abuse remains stamped on the victim's libido in such a way that, unconsciously and in spite of hating it, she wants to repeat it. If the abuse remains a secret, it can repeat for generations. I have seen genealogy trees where the grandmother was raped—as was the daughter, as was the granddaughter.) Adults who were seduced by their fathers seek out lovers who represent them. The pleasure they had when they were children was not sexual but rather sensual. What remains in her mind is to obtain a satiation that she did not experience at the time of the abuse when the orgasm was reserved for her father. She is not only possessed physically but also psychically. If the consultant wants to free herself, I recommend:

- The consultant goes to a church and tells a priest all of the crudest details of the sexual acts with her father. She should exaggerate and invent to the maximum, telling him that her father made her masturbate him and lick his penis, that he penetrated her vaginally and anally, that he urinated in her mouth, ejaculated in her face, and defecated on her stomach. When the priest is shocked, she should tell him in a hoarse voice and with a demonic expression that she is ready to repeat the experience with him. Leaving the church, she should go to a bakery and devour six cakes. Then she should dress from head to foot in new clothes and change her name.

- If a cynical brother (or some other relative) has abused the consultant when she was little and now refuses to admit this when confronted, saying that her memories are false, the consultant, in order to free herself from the victim's rage, should put a bull's testicles stained with blood (which can be fake) in a plastic bag and mail it to him.

A consultant told me, "My father abused me, but he is dead. How do I free myself from this?" I responded:

- "Take a one-foot-long, thick chain to your kitchen and use it to break all of the plates, glasses, jars, trays—everything." The touched woman said, "Incredible! The crockery I use is the only inheritance my father gave me." "Break it all! And bury the pieces. Over the burial place, plant a tree together with a vine, so the healthy link with your father will be fulfilled in this vegetation."

When a boy has been his father's sexual victim, hemorrhoids may appear in adulthood along with a lack of confidence in his virility, difficulty concentrating, a constant feeling of cowardice, difficulty maturing, timidity with women, homosexual fantasies that excite him when he masturbates, and so forth. To free himself from all of this, the consultant should carry out the following act:

- The consultant buys the biggest sausage possible, drills a hole through it lengthwise, and fills it with condensed milk. On a flat rock, the consultant sticks a photograph of his father to his own excrement and places the prepared sausage on top of it. Then the consultant attacks this with an ax until it is in pieces, while screaming and releasing all of his painful rage. He sends the pieces to his father by mail. If his father is dead, the consultant leaves them at his father's grave. The consultant buries the ax and plants an olive tree over it.

63. LOVESICKNESS

Lovesickness is not cured through advice. The inconsolable person, whose heart is broken, suffers from the pain of being abandoned or rejected by someone he loves and does not listen to reason. What purpose does it serve to tell the person that he does not really suffer for whom he thinks he suffers but rather he projects onto this person an abandonment from childhood—a sadness felt from a belief of having lost the mother's love at some point in his childhood? The child, before developing his individuality, feels like a part of his mother—she is his essential "I"; if he loses her, he loses part of himself. When the consultant is an adult, he projects this dependent affection onto the object of his love. In order to free himself from this breakup and begin his emotional life again, the mourner should make a big effort to say, "I am not the one suffering: my inner child is suffering."

Our eating habits most physically bind us to our childhoods: a big part of what we eat unites us to the past. In the case of a broken heart, I recommend:

- The consultant radically changes his eating habits. If he is a carnivore, he should become vegetarians, or vice versa. If the consultant does not live near the seashore, he should travel to one and spend three days there. He should take up jogging on the beach, dipping his feet in the water, and repeating, "Pain, you are not mine." During this time period, the consultant will carry on his back, at all times, a calf's heart in a plastic bag along with a photograph of his lost lover and a photograph of his mother. After these three days, the consultant will bury the heart and plant an apple tree over it. (The same act is valid for female consultants, but instead of using feminine photographs, she should use their masculine equivalents.)

If, in spite of this, the consultant continues to suffer, he will have to gather all of his strength to decide to change his heart metaphorically.

▶ With the windows covered with a thick curtain, the consultant, at midnight, lies naked on the floor in his bedroom surrounded by a circle of twelve lit candles. The consultant glues to his heart with honey a photograph of the beloved and, on top of that, seven saucers. For a quarter of an hour, the consultant pushes this pillar of plates against his chest as though wanting to embed them. Then, with a little hammer, the consultant begins to break them, one by one—not with only one blow but with a progressive effort, first with soft blows then with one final blow, repeated seven times.

Meanwhile, the consultant expresses his pain with the most intense screaming and wailing possible. When the photograph is finally exposed, the consultant pours a little artificial blood over it (prepared beforehand by the consultant himself, by mixing red food coloring with a warmed sex lubricant). Feeling that the photograph has roots in his heart, the consultant simulates struggling to pluck it out, until, with a triumphant exclamation, he withdraws it from his chest. The consultant crumples up the photograph into a ball. Then the consultant cleans up the blood with a cloth on which an image of the Virgin Mary is printed. The consultant then rubs the heart region with half a lemon.

Finally, the consultant puts the crumpled photograph, the hammer, the pieces of broken saucer, the used lemon, the bottle of fake blood, and the burned-out candles into a bag. The consultant puts the cloth under his mattress, then paints his face and hands with silver costume paint, goes out on the street, and throws the bag in the first trash bin he finds. Then, still in the silver paint, the consultant goes to a bar to celebrate and get drunk.

64. FEAR OF FINANCIAL FAILURE

Some poorly interpreted phrases from the Gospels (like, for example, "Blessed are the poor" or "It is easier for a camel to go through the eye of a needle than for a rich man to enter into the kingdom of God") encourage the power of the wealthy and keep those most in need in a position of submission. People who have problems with money (chronic debtors, compulsive spenders, those with a chronic attitude or bearing of failure) are possessed by family beliefs that were inculcated during childhood ("For ye know the grace of our Lord Jesus Christ, that, though he was rich, yet for your sakes he became poor"), which drive these people to self-sabotage: "I don't have the right," "I don't deserve it," "Why me?" "I have no value," "I am to blame," "Money is disgusting."

Actually, society functions mainly by spreading the constant message of economic terror among its citizens. The fear of not having anything to eat or of not having anywhere to live is spread through the fear of sickness, the fear of aging, the fear of being attacked, and, from there, the fear of not being loved, the fear of loneliness, the fear of being dissolved into oblivion. This anxiety of "lack" or "shortage" (that there is never enough) produces a thirst to consume (albeit on credit!). All consumption produces waste, excrement, and the unconscious makes a pairing of the concepts of wealth and waste. So to the consultants who suffer from this morbid economic fear, I foremost advise:

- The consultant dresses up in the most elegant way possible (tie pin, designer sunglasses, flamboyant wristwatch, jewelry, carrying a fine cigar) and begs in public. He begs money from drivers and from people passing on the street. Meanwhile, the consultant holds, in one hand, a cardboard sign that reads, "'Ask, and it shall be given. —Saint Matthew' I am afraid that I lack everything." Then the consultant buys four gold coins and inserts them into his anus, keeping them there for four days. Then the consultant defecates in a urinal and rescues the four coins. Just as they are, the consultant buries them in a pot beneath flowers that require daily watering. Furthermore, for the next forty nights, before going to bed, the consultant has a full-body massage, which he pays for with a $500 bill that he has borrowed from one of his parents. (If the parents are absent or dead, the consultant uses his own bill, folded in two and containing a photo of his parents.)

65. FEAR OF AGING

Our society, every day becoming less mature, worships youth and also instills a contempt for old age. For the past sixty years, with retirement, society has begun to exclude its citizens from social activity. Formerly, society associated male old age with wisdom: today, it is confused with decadence. For women, the problem is worse: not only are women excluded from wisdom (in popular traditions and stories, the old woman is almost always an old witch) but also from the life of love. This causes an ancestral fear: that of being excluded from the tribe and from life and, moreover, that of being rejected by the whole world. My recommendation for a consultant affected by this anguish is based on a Persian proverb: "Whatever you do at night, do first in the morning."

▶ The consultant hires a professional makeup artist to make up her face, using hyperrealistic makeup to make the consultant look ninety years old. The consultant spends a whole day with this "look." From morning until night, the consultant sits in a café or in a public square speaking with young people, and in this way, the consultant will see life from another point of view: the reality that, in fact, when she grows old, there will be a place for her.

66. FEAR OF FAINTING

If the consultant has a fear of vertigo or dizziness that is due to something psychological but does not want to undergo psychotherapy, I recommend the consultant train in a new martial art called ukemido, which contains the word *ukemi,* meaning "to fall" in Japanese. Children experience pleasure in letting themselves fall. Adults, however, consider falling to be a humiliation. In martial arts, one always studies a fall with the intention not of staying on the ground but of rolling and getting up as quickly as possible in order to continue the fight. "To fall" is always accompanied with "getting up": love of the floor has been eliminated. To defeat this neurosis, I propose:

- The consultant, separating herself from all false dignity, should abandon herself to the call of gravity and allow herself to fall in order to then wallow on the floor in pleasure. One can do this anywhere: at home, in the home of a friend or relative, at a party, at a professional meeting. Then the consultant may invite her partner to fall while embracing, and then the consultant's friends, children, parents. A whole family, letting themselves fall, will obtain a healing moment of happiness. Once quiet, lying on the ground, the fallen ones can engage in peaceful conversations.

I received this solicitation for help:

Ten years ago, I had a respiratory panic/anxiety attack. I have not had another one, but since then I have not been able to free myself from fear of the attack, which was horrible, happening again. What psychomagic act do you recommend?

I replied:

- The consultant goes to a supermarket at a very busy time of day and fakes an anxiety/panic attack, letting himself fall on the floor. When people offer help, the consultant asks for a glass of milk, saying that it is the only thing that can calm him down. As soon as the consultant drinks the milk, he smiles and takes off running. He then goes to a sex shop, buys a porn magazine, and, seated on the terrace of a café, openly looks at the lewd images.

67. FEAR OF THE DARK

When some people are alone, they sleep with the lights on because of a fear of the dark. This nocturnal terror comes from childhood. If, at any moment, the consultant's parents went out at night, and the little one woke up alone and surrounded by huge shadows, then the consultant, feeling abandoned, defenseless, and in danger of an imminent attack by some unknown, will feel smothered by this burden for much of her life. To this consultant, I explain that the scary shadows are repressed wishes of her personality that wish to manifest. Then I recommend the following:

- The consultant should imagine that the shadows are big threads that are interwoven to make fabric. At the same time, with black wool and needles, the consultant should sew a vest. If the consultant does not know how to sew, he will learn to sew, leaving aside any notion that sewing is "only for women" or "not for me." (Sailors sew!) Once the vest is finished, the consultant incorporates other black garments with it and also paints his face and hands black, thus becoming part of the darkness. The consultant then walks around the unlit house feeling nighttime turn into an ally. This will help the consultant—understanding that the unconscious is an ally—to let the repressed aspects of his personality express themselves.

68. FEAR OF INSANITY

Fear of insanity withdraws reality from the sufferer. Therefore, I recommend:

- The consultant makes a hat lined with lead and uses shoes with soles made from the same heavy metal. The weight of the hat and the shoes will force him to be present with each step he takes and with each thought he has. Beneath the hat, the consultant will put a photograph of himself in which he is grinning like a madman. The consultant walks around like that. Three days later, he buries the shoes and the hat and plants a lavender bush on top. Then he rolls up the photograph and sends it to the sky by attaching it to three helium balloons and letting go of the balloons in the open air.

69. SPELLS FOR FEAR

Through the family network (psychological legacy of the parents, aunts and uncles, grandparents and great-grandparents), the past will exert a negative effect over the individual, inviting her to repeat crazy ideas, dissatisfactions, traumas, illnesses, deaths, divorce, and financial terrors or failures. If the consultant wants to develop a broader level of consciousness than that of the clan, she will have to observe the repetitions that either threaten or have already been repeated with corresponding doses of suffering and anguish. The consultant's quest for inner peace will allow her to accept the emotional and moral pain, which comes from searching the memory for the errors and abuse to which the consultant was subjected. This important introspection will find the consultant constrained by different fears that will affect her lucidity, pushing her to enclose herself in the limited "I" that integrates her in the clan. Thus, the consultant should abandon her identification with this personality instilled by the family, society, and the culture and, instead, devote herself to her essential being in constant evolution. It is precisely this surrender to the essential being that drives the consultant to trust the unconscious, no longer considering it an enemy but rather an ally, and accepting that in the deepest part of darkness there is a shining and all-powerful point—united with the universal energy and the divine consciousness, which one may call the inner God. In the Gospel of Luke, when the Angel Gabriel appeared before the Virgin, the first thing he said after a greeting was, "Fear not, Mary: for you have found favor with God." This can be understood psychologically as meaning that Gabriel (the essential being) asks Maria (ego in a state of grace, union with totality) to surrender to the transmuting action of her inner God (the only dimension of the psyche capable of overcoming all fears).

Importance was always given to words in old magic traditions, such that, when a magician battles illnesses, he recites spells. And religions make use of prayers, orations recited aloud, vows, mantras, and so forth. The constant repetition of certain sacred words calms the mind, releasing it from the vicious cycle of its continuous inner dialogue. A new idea repeated with faith and will can open doors in a mental prison, causing the needed liberating mutation.

▶ Each time fear afflicts the consultant, these are the psychomagic spells she should repeat aloud:

> *Fear . . .*
> *of change:*
> *to advance on the path of consciousness, I must accept the death of the concepts I have of myself.*
>
> *of desire:*
> *sexual energy is sacred. I must quit rejecting and hiding myself.*

of getting sick:
physical illnesses are teachers that can cure my soul sicknesses.

of aging:
time is my ally. It brings me wisdom.

of failure:
everything is failure because nothing is eternal. The only true success is the achievement of consciousness.

of humiliation:
if I overcome my pride, no one can humiliate me.

of darkness:
the night is always united with the day.

of poverty:
the creativity of the essential being is my wealth.

of loneliness:
if I open myself to the world, everything accompanies me.

of violence:
I will overcome my own aggression, I will stop projecting my anger into the world.

of death:
death is an illusion of the individual ego. I am part of the universe that is eternal and infinite. I will exist forever in some form or another.

of not being able to communicate:
my inner God knows every language.

of being unable to resist the truth:
truth destroys suffering in me. Suffering is caused by what I am not, the barriers erected by the past. I will quit asserting my ego; I will give it to my essential being.

of not progressing:
if I identify with the universe, I unite with its incessant expansion.

of not being desired:
the universe has given me the strength of birth. Divine consciousness loves me.

of not being logical:
the universe does not obey logical laws; the "logic" of the human brain is "insanity" for the universe.

of losing the definition:
the sum of all definitions is my definition, including the nondefinition defining me.

of losing my identity:
my ego's boundaries are only useful for a certain amount of time; I should not hang on to them, believing they are my identity. My mind, obeying the projections of the future, will fight to expand until it arrives at being what it is: cosmic consciousness.

of losing personal seduction:
if I free myself from my desires then seduction will become useless to me.

of losing my capabilities:
my inner God is inextinguishable.

of losing a battle:
losing a battle is not losing myself.

of being forced into silence:
if I have something to say, I will say it in the world; if I can't say it in the world, I will say it in my country; if I can't say it in my country, I will say it in my city; if I can't say it in my city, I will say it in my home; if I can't say it in my home, I will say it to myself: humans form a whole and whatever I say to myself, I say to the collective unconsciousness.

of being robbed:
whatever anyone can steal from me was never mine. The essential being is permanent.

of being disappointed by love:
my emotional certainty is to love without asking to be loved.

of being disfigured:
I don't identify myself with my face. I will integrate myself in the impersonality of my indestructible essential being.

of being incarcerated:
they can only incarcerate my body.

of being barren:
at every moment, infinity inseminates me. The soul is my supreme daughter.

of being wounded, of having an amputation, of being physically handicapped:
I am a spirit that has a body and not a body that has a spirit. Even if I lose my whole body, I will continue to exist in another dimension.

of being invaded:
I am infinite. The universe is my body.

of being raped:
vexing my body does not dirty my soul.

of emptiness:
if I stop identifying myself with my ego (the emptiness into which I am afraid of falling), my essential being will fall into me.

70. CAREER TROUBLE

Psychomagic is not intended to act on the minds of others in order to force the fulfillment of undesirable acts. That is called magic, be that white or black. One heals oneself; the other tries to change someone else without having changed oneself first. For example:

1. Protection against Envious Peers

Magic advises us to carry an image of Chango, the African god of fire, with us in order to absorb the powers of envy and to transform them to our favor. Psychomagic, on the other hand, advises the consultant (who cannot work in peace because he or she is aware of peer envy) to accept that the world is what it is: the world is more than what the consultant thinks it is. The envy the consultant feels coming from others is actually partly coming from the outside and partly coming from the inside. The only way to transform the envy is to respond to it with love instead of reflecting it into the world. For this, I recommend:

- The consultant should have big hearts printed on the front and back of a camisole that she wears underneath her blouse or T-shirt. This way, in the middle of a sandwich of hearts, the consultant will be immune to such bad vibrations. If the consultant has collaborators, have them also wear this kind of protective shirt and keep it a secret, sowing love wherever they go.

2. Protection against Enemies at Work

Magic proposes that we take some person's dear object, which the person always has on his table, and then bewitch it. We constantly use it while reciting spells, then we return the object to the person's worktable. If, however, we employ psychomagic, then we investigate the consultant's past:

- The consultant makes a list of all of his enemies, from the most recent to the oldest—it is possible to find them as far back as grade school or else embodied in the family as a brother or sister or some other relative and even a stepparent. The consultant will understand, therefore, that the exterior enemies are, in large part, projections of the enemies we keep in our memory. So that the hostility ends, the consultant will have to make nice efforts toward his "enemy": for fifteen continuous days, the consultant will anonymously place a white rose on the person's worktable.

3. *Get a Promotion*

Magic proposes that we take a bird's tongue and recite over it, "Your silver song, thou has sung for my safe future." Then burn a silver candle and spread the ashes underneath our boss's seat. Clearly, if we are superstitious, we will believe that the tongue of this poor bird (which we killed) will turn into a watery ghost that will come along to whistle a tune in our boss's ears as he discusses the coveted promotion and points to our own personal, excellent skills and qualifications. From a psychomagic point of view, we confirm and accept that all promotions have a political aspect: there will generally be one boss who defends us in front of another boss who is defending someone else, some other choice. Each side fights by deploying his or her power. A defeat (which is, for us, a social failure) eats away at our self-esteem. More important than getting a promotion is being prepared to win without falling upon an excess of vanity or, with the other outcome, lose without feeling ashamed.

▶ The female consultant, on promotion day, will write on a little piece of parchment paper, in red ink with a drop of blood added to it, "I am worthy! I can do it!" The consultant will then roll the paper up and insert it into her vagina. Whatever the result is, she will bury this paper in a potted plant, which she will place on her desk. The male consultant, on promotion day, will wrap around his penis a golden ribbon on which he has written, "I am worthy! I can do it!" No matter the results, he will bury the ribbon in a potted plant, which he will place on his desk.

4. *Win a Labor Litigation*

Magic recommends that we send the antagonistic boss a dead fly pierced by a pin after reciting over it, "Look at the evil you do. Let it turn against you." In psychomagic, this is an act of aggression that only adds hate to hate. Labor litigation is an unpleasant matter that can turn into something seriously dangerous for our professional career. If, after a confrontation, our boss is not able to forgive us, he or she will make our work life unbearable. The best advice is to stay out of conflicts. But if we fail to do so, I recommend:

- The consultant will send to the adversary a bottle of champagne and a bouquet of white roses with the following note, "You have your reasons; I understand them. And I have mine; I hope you understand them. Whatever the result of this conflict, my admiration for your human and professional qualities will not change."

5. *Make a Good Impression in a New Job*

We must remain distant but cordial. Magic advises that we carry turquoise in our pocket for the first days. Whenever we are asked our opinion on a thorny issue, we touch this turquoise and respond that we are not yet clear enough to articulate an opinion on the matter. In this case, psychomagic agrees with magic. But, not being superstition, psychomagic considers awarding powers to a stone can add to our pride, making us believe we have superpowers. I therefore recommend:

- The consultant, instead of turquoise, carries dog excrement in a plastic tube onto which he has pasted a sticker that reads, "I am not prideful."

6. *Make My Boss Stop Criticizing Me*

Magic proposes that we put a dead spider somewhere in the boss's desk where the cleaning people won't find it, and we recite, "The incomprehension of [name] will be entangled in this web and [name] will understand my point of view and stop tormenting me." This act turns the person involved into a coward because, under the pretext of working on himself, the consultant is trying to change the mind of some other. Psychomagic proposes that the affected person examines the relationships he had during childhood with parents and teachers: most likely they severely criticized the consultant. It is also possible that, realizing that his mistakes attracted attention, he has painstakingly repeated them and chews on the grudge—a grudge that may be intuitively perceived by the censor, increasing the reproaches. Therefore, I recommend:

- For each of the boss's criticisms, the consultant deposits in a piggy bank placed on the consultant's desk a $5 or $10 bill. Once a month, he will take the accumulated money to purchase something to please the boss and leave it anonymously in the boss's office. This will prevent ruminating on resentments. In this way, the consultant becomes more pleasant, and the boss's unconscious desire to criticize the consultant will be eliminated.

7. Become Autonomous and Create My Own Company

Magic suggests we have an amulet capable of providing us with a lot of luck. For example, over a horseshoe recite, "Do me lucky favors! Grant me prosperity!" Then we should hang this horseshoe upside down above the door and inside of the place where we are going to work. During a psychomagic consultation, although the consultant may love not feeling tied to another's schedule and can use time for eating or resting without being rushed, we analyze the degree of economic insecurity that the absence of a fixed salary causes in the person who wants to make herself autonomous. In the depths of the unconscious, the character we acquired during childhood prevails. In most families, the children are not taught to manage money or to open a bank account, nor are they given financial rewards. As adults (actually dependent children), in order to enjoy a steady income, they continue looking for work that is, most of the time, unsatisfying. They have not learned to invest. They are terrified of taking risks. One of surrealism's main slogans is "Leave the safe for the uncertain."

▶ The best way to become a freelancer is to develop the ability to make money. First, invest one's resources in small, new, absolutely uncertain, authentic, and completely extravagant businesses; manage to make enough daily bread from something through which it seemed totally impossible to earn a penny.

If the consultant achieves this, she will be strengthened and able to take risks in better businesses without needing to nail a horseshoe to the door, understanding that good luck is not something one receives like manna fallen from the sky, but rather, in order to have it, one must be capable of making it by courageous investments.

Examples of little businesses:

1. Just like children make puppets and all kinds of objects to then paint, organize workshops in which, as a meditation, participants paint figurines of Buddha and other gods.
2. Collaborate with a veterinarian to give massages to cats.
3. Provide a psychological cleaning service using a bundle of herbs and holy water to clean psychic residue from the sofas and chairs in psychological clinics.
4. Provide rehabilitation classes for the phantom limbs of maimed people.
5. Taking into account the brain's ability to respond to placebos, give acupuncture treatments, sticking needles into patients' shadows.
6. Dressed as a Franciscan monk, stating that pets have souls, baptize dogs, cats, parrots, white mice, and so forth, according to Christian rite, to save their souls and to allow them to enter paradise.
7. On the basis that people with bald heads retain a memory of their lost hair, become a hairstylist that washes and styles the invisible strands.

If the consultant manages to earn money through these kinds of quirky trades, she will be prepared for success in arranging a serious and independent business.

71. FRIGIDITY

In the collective unconscious, mythology remains active and can act, in a subtle way, on our reality. Even though we have forgotten the language of symbols, they influence our behavior. The peacock, for the old Christians, was the symbol of resurrection: as winter approaches, the tail loses its feathers but, as spring arrives, the feathers return. With this tail full of "eyes," the male circles the female and holds her spellbound. The feathers are heavy with sexual charms.

A woman experiences frigidity as if something inside her were dead. This is why her lack of pleasure is compared with the coldness of cadavers. Therefore, I recommend:

► The consultant, before making love, asks her lover to caress her sex with peacock feathers for a half hour. Then she will feel the rebirth of her capacity for pleasure. When she is penetrated, and as the man makes his pelvic motions, she should crack raw eggs on his head, one by one, exclaiming, "Take that!"

If, after having smashed ten eggs, she has not had an orgasm, she should simulate an orgasm in the most exaggerated possible way and then for seven days—upon awaking in the morning and at night before going to bed—she should repeat this simulation.

72. NEGATIVE FORECASTING

As was said in the beginning of section one, parents etch threatening words into their children's memory. These orders to not do something later turn into the desire to do it because the brain tends to fulfill predictions. All predictions act like curses. If parents tell a little girl who is playing with her sex, "Quit doing that or else, when you are older, you will turn into a whore," when she is an adult, the urge to be a prostitute may obsess her. The only way to be freed from a prediction is to fulfill it metaphorically. Below are some examples.

A person had a Tarot reading. The reader said, "Someone close to you will die, and this is going to cost you a lot of money." The person, obsessed, turned to me for guidance. I recommended the following:

- ▶ The consultant closes the windows, sprays insecticide, and waits until a fly dies. This means the prediction "Someone close to you will die" has been fulfilled. The consultant takes a $5 bill, adds six zeros to it (turning it into a $5 million bill), rolls up the fly, then buries it, fulfilling the prediction "This is going to cost you a lot of money," and the consultant is freed from the anguish.

A female psychologist, the daughter and granddaughter of psychologists, who, when she was little, wanted to be a ballerina but who, later, decided to follow the family trade, came to me because, in spite of having many patients, she suffered permanent economic anxiety. She remembered that her mother had repeatedly insisted, "Life is very hard, my daughter. If you don't follow in the professional footsteps of your father and grandfather, you will end up sleeping on the street like those drunken beggars when you are older." To be rid of this prediction, I recommended:

- ▶ For ten days, the consultant meets her patients dressed as a tattered beggar, with her nose painted red and carrying a bottle of wine and a piece of cheese around with her.

She was afraid that her patients would think she was crazy, so I told her she could stop it by telling them she was fulfilling a psychomagic act. This she did, and at the end of ten days her economic anxiety ended.

73. DISSATISFACTION WITH PHYSICAL APPEARANCE

Many people have surgery to change their facial features. They believe they do it for aesthetic reasons. However, this desire for change conceals a deeper problem than that of a simple search for beauty. If a person is not satisfied with his or her face, it means the mother or father (or both) were dissatisfied with their child's face.

If the parents form a narcissistic couple, each will want the offspring to take after him or her. It may be that the mother conceived a child with a man whom she did not love, who disappeared, or whom she hated. If the child looks like her, she will love the child. If the child looks like the father, she will turn into an emotionally cold or indifferent mother with a just barely concealed aggressiveness.

If the father or mother does not resolve his or her incestuous urges, he or she will want the offspring to look like the loved grandfather or grandmother, and if this is not the case, then the parent will not give love to the offspring. A child is not beautiful or ugly in an abstract way based on any aesthetic canon: he or she is beautiful if the clan's familiar features are present. If all the relatives have big noses and the child possesses a small one, the child will be considered ugly, which is to say, like a foreigner. Whoever suffers this excommunication grows up lacking self-esteem, feeling empty inside, needing to continuously look in the mirror of others to know who he is, and discovering a bad image of himself, he feels the need to mask it and to conceal it. His neurotic personality is born of an injustice, an abuse, a wound that has interfered with the first stages of development when, during conception, his mother having been overwhelmed by a man, resentment, pain, rage, and fear were transferred to him.

A reader sent me this e-mail:

> I suffer from a continuous need to know the state of my face.

> When I look at myself in the mirror, I feel a horrible tension: it is as if my face will remain as it is in my mind, like a photograph. This sick discomfort with my face is very awkward. I can hardly socialize. I also feel that it is very difficult to be an adult (I am forty-seven), always obsessed with the passage of time, with feelings of depersonalization. I have tried all kinds of therapy without good results. Help me.

To the causes we have described, we can add to this case (from a Freudian point of view) a fixation or detention in the person's development at the infant stages of deep gratification. If the mother hates men, the person affected will try to remain a child and never mature, unable as it were to tolerate and to cope with the challenges and failures that adulthood and life entails. I recommend:

- The consultant puts a fancy gilt frame on his mirror. A professional makeup artist for film should make a mold of his face, which is then used to make ten hyperrealistic papier-mâché masks. The consultant paints his face gold and wears one of these masks from morning until night, removing it only to eat and to bathe. Before bed and in front of a mirror while listening to a recording of music the consultant thinks is sublime, he removes the mask and puts a grape-flavored lozenge in his mouth. Always looking at himself in the mirror, he places the mask in a basin and sets it on fire. He carefully puts the ashes in a metal box. He repeats this act ten days in a row. On the tenth day, he goes out—to work, shopping, sightseeing—with his gold-painted face. He sends the box of ashes to his mother.

If this problem occurs in a woman, she should see if the heartbreak is with the father or the mother and act according to the trauma.

74. MARITAL BOREDOM

Some married women feel urges to make love with other men, but they suppress the urges because their moral upbringing prohibits infidelity. Husbands may feel the same way. I recommend:

- The consultant reserves a hotel room and tells her partner, "I have a dentist appointment. I'll be back later." The consultant goes to this hotel room and dresses in very seductive clothes (prostitute style) that she has taken there beforehand, and waits. An unknown man arrives—it can be a construction worker, a rock musician, a soldier (actually, her husband in disguise)—and, without saying a word, they make love. He gives her money and leaves. The consultant gets back into her normal clothes and gives her husband time to get back home and remove his costume. When the consultant arrives home, the husband asks her, "Where have you been?" The consultant responds, "I already told you. I had a dentist appointment."

  The couple can repeat this act wearing different disguises each time.

75. THE WOMAN BOUND TO HER EX-LOVER

Some women, in spite of having separated from their lovers, have a hard time beginning a new life with a new partner. Without loving the men who left them, there is something mysterious still attracting them to these men. I thus recommend:

- The consultant, for six days in a row, an hour each day, should carry her house key in her vagina. After the sixth time doing this, the consultant will send this key by mail to her former lover then change the locks.

76. PRESERVING LOVE AND FRIENDSHIP

It is common for someone in love, or who has the privilege of finding a faithful or unselfish friend, to fear for whatever reason the emotional bond breaking. In the delights of love and friendship, anxiety over no longer being loved or wanted always appears. This comes from early childhood. However much a mother strives to meet the demands of her baby, sometimes it takes time. Most of the time, the child is not crying from hunger but from the anxiety over believing herself abandoned; a few minutes to an adult are a few minutes, but for an infant, each minute seems to last for hours. The consultant, even though reason tells her there is no reason that the relationship is in danger, receives from her unconscious messages of insecurity. In order to calm her down, the consultant should fulfill one or both of the following acts recommended by popular sorcerers, which will prove to the consultant that the bond is solid. (All of the details that seem absurd due to its ceremonial nature will convince the unconscious that the amorous or friendly ties are solid.)

- The consultant pricks the index finger with a pin and lets some drops of blood fall on a little mirror. With a feather from a black hen, the consultant writes on parchment paper the first and last names of the person whose love the consultant wishes to keep. The just-drawn blood will serve as ink. The consultant tightly wraps the parchment paper around a red candle and binds it with green thread. Between midnight and 2 a.m. on Friday, the consultant burns the candle.

  The consultant grabs a handful of herbs and holds them between her lips with pieces sticking out. The consultant kneels down facing east and thinks about her lover or friend for a few minutes. The consultant then takes the herbs with the left hand and, holding them up, says, "Together at dawn." Then the consultant puts the herbs back in her mouth, kneels facing west, and thinks again about the loved friend. Then the consultant holds the herbs in the right hand, gets up, and says, "Together at sunset." The consultant keeps the herbs and uses them in any food she and her loved friend eat together.

77. RELATIONSHIP CONFLICTS

Individuals, caught in the trap of their genealogy trees, tend to repeatedly copy their parents, unconsciously seeking to relive childhood suffering. Thus, a daughter of an often absent father may fall in love with a man who lives in a distant city, or the son of an apathetic mother may look only for women who are unable to love. When others do not correspond to their neurotic projections, they pass them by without any interest. Conversely, if the neuroses match, there is an immediate attraction. The "lovers" each pretend to be what the other wants in order to be mutually desirable. But there is a point at which the differences are perceived, and unable to tolerate this, the couple begins to fight. What has happened? Each wanted in someone else what he or she lacked in him- or herself.

For example: he shows certain intellectual cunning and sexual vigor, but he is blocked in the expression of his emotions, and he doesn't know how to handle everyday life. On the other hand, she can easily organize her daily life and express her feelings, but she is frigid, and she suffers with intellectual insecurity. Uniting their fulfilled parts—he, the intellectual and sexual; she, the materialistic and emotional—they are balanced. But, by connecting their complexes—his material and emotional insecurity and her intellectual and sexual inferiority—they plunge into serious struggles where each one must complete something of the other, and meanwhile each one is waiting to be completed by the other. They will never get complete satisfaction. The place they occupy is not for two but for one.

Essentially, there are four kinds of conflicts: struggle to exist, struggle for sexual identity, struggle for satisfaction, struggle for power.

The Mexicans have a saying, "According to how the toad is, so is the stone," which means a big problem requires a broad solution. If the consultants are submerged in one of the four battles and are able to look at it fearlessly, recognizing the neurotic ties uniting them and understanding that a perfect partnership is not born through a spontaneous generation but is obtained by applying the same energy used to create a work of art, then I recommend that they dedicate six consecutive days to a series of psychomagic acts.

1. Struggle to Exist

Since my parents did not give me enough attention and did not value me, I have been unable to form "I." I do not know who or how I am. I feel empty. Life doesn't make sense to me. I am worthless. I will give myself completely to you because I am not even worth pretending to be of value. You are all that exists in my world. My happiness is in your hands.

Someone like this is a living trap: an adult who, with the anxiety of an abandoned baby, waits for the partner to say, "You exist!" The being who feels empty finds another who also feels empty. One is passive ("I give myself to you; you will be my 'I'"), while the other is active ("I accept: thanks to you, I will fill up my emptiness feeling like I am somebody; I will become your ideal").

In the beginning, one worships and the other allows the worship. Gradually, the humble will manipulate the prideful until the humble one ends up the director. And one day—having acquired the necessary security—the formerly humble one will demolish the idol's pedestal, making it fall down: "Now I am you and you are me and, because of this, I despise you. I will find another who merits my admiration." For the consultants caught in this struggle, I recommend:

- **Monday:** The male consultant dresses like a boy of no more than seven years and talks and acts as such. His wife plays the part of an older lady, wearing a medallion around the neck with a photograph of his mother. The whole day, she treats him as a mature, affectionate woman would treat her son: she caresses him, she feeds him what he wants to eat, she glorifies his beauty and value, she accompanies him to meet his needs, she takes him out for a walk (in costume), she plays with him, and, finally (always in character), they sleep very close to one another without making love.

- **Tuesday:** The female consultant dresses like a girl of no more than seven years and talks and acts as such. Her husband plays the part of an older man, wearing a medallion around the neck with a photograph of the wife's father. The whole day, he treats her like a mature, affectionate man would treat his daughter: he caresses her, he gives her what she wants to eat, he glorifies her beauty and value, he accompanies her to meet her needs, he takes her out for a walk (in costume), he plays games with her, and, finally (always in character), they sleep very close to one another without making love.

- **Wednesday:** Both, dressed like children, spend the day playing and making mischief. Hand in hand, they go to the cinema to see a child's animation film. They eat only pastries, and finally (always in character), they will sleep closely together, tenderly, without making love.

- **Thursday:** Both act like adults. Him (as a woman) dressed up as his own mother and her (as a man) dressed up as her own father. They spend the whole day imitating these characters with all of their mistakes and limitations. They sleep separately during the night.

- **Friday:** Now without costume, they do not talk for the whole day. They share time and meals in silence. At night, they undress and caress one another. He adopts the seated position and she embraces him from the front. The penis will penetrate the vagina, this way; intimately united, they do not move. Uniting their voices, they recite the following text, which will be memorized: "Trust me. I never want you to judge or compare me; I want you to realize I am unique. In the depths of my being there is something that has never imitated anyone: something that only you can see because I am what you were always waiting for. I want you to reveal all your secrets to me because I won't keep any secrets from you. I was dead; you resurrected me. By recognizing me, you have revealed me to myself. I will never go back to being what they made me believe I was. As a single flower that opens, together we will continue expanding the boundaries of our consciousness."

- **Saturday:** The man and woman invite friends and relatives to join them in celebration of their marriage (or the renewed marriage if they are already married). The couple, bound at the wrists with a pair of handcuffs and otherwise completely naked, greets the friends and relatives and behave naturally, as if they are dressed. There will be an intimate ceremony during which a previously chosen (in mutual agreement) guest reads a marriage contract, and both sign it with drops of blood drawn from their ring fingers. (The marriage contract is shown at the end of this chapter, on pages 127–28.)

2. Struggle for Sexual Identity

The woman feels a deep desire to conquer masculinity; the man, to express his femininity. She simulates a femininity she doesn't know because her mother was manly. He simulates a virility he doesn't know because he had an absent or weak father: he was raised by his mother or grandmother or another female relative. As time passes, they remove their masks: the woman begins to act like the man and the man the woman. When she does whatever she pleases, he locks himself in passivity. She progressively becomes frigid. It becomes increasingly difficult for him to get an erection. Both have lost desire. For things to run smoothly, she needs to lose respect for him. But, if she loses respect for him, his impotence persists. For the consultants caught in this struggle, I recommend:

- **Monday:** She dresses up like a little girl of no more than seven years and behaves and talks as such. He plays the role of a mature, older lady wearing a medallion around his neck with a photograph of her mother. The whole day, he treats her like a virile woman would treat her daughter—not a lot of caresses, fast food, criticisms that devalue her femininity—and accompanies her throughout the day while she does what she needs to do. Then he takes her bowling. Finally, they sleep separately in their costumes.

- **Tuesday:** He dresses up like a little boy of no more than seven years and behaves and talks as such. She plays the role of a mature, older man wearing a medallion around her neck with a photograph of his father. The whole day, she treat hims like a feminine and weak man would treat his son: combing his hair so he is beautiful, having him help clean the house and cook, teaching him to urinate while seated, taking him out for a walk (in costume). They admire the shop windows, and she plays dolls with him. Finally, they sleep very closely together without making love.

- **Wednesday:** Both dress as children—him as a girl, her as a boy—and spend the day playing together and making mischief. They go hand in hand to the cinema to watch a children's movie, they only eat pastries, and finally, still playing the roles of the characters, they sleep closely together, tenderly, without making love.

- **Thursday:** Each plays an adult: him (as a woman) dressed in his wife's clothes and her (as a man) dressed in her husband's clothes. They spend the day imitating the other, with all their errors and limitations. At night, they sleep separately.

- **Friday:** Now without any costumes they spend the day in silence. They spend time and meals in silence. At night they undress and caress one another. She kneels, he gets close from the back and penetrates her. Intimately united like this, they do not move. Uniting their voices, they recite the following text by memory: "I appreciate your existence. I want you to consider my mind and body as your own. I want you to give yourself to me with the hope that we will merge into a simultaneous orgasm: a common objective. I want you to channel your sacred animal and turn me into its only objective. I want you to feel, through my imperfections, the beauty of the divine perfection, because in our ovaries and testicles resides the project of a perfect humanity. The pleasure of our embraces will be condensed into children who will be our builders; delivering ourselves to each other will allow innumerable descendants to populate the galaxies. You, the totality of all of my knowledge and mystery; you, the bright peak of my pleasure."

- **Saturday:** Inviting friends and relatives to celebrate the marriage (a new wedding if the couple is already married), the couple greets the guests bound at the wrists with a pair of handcuffs and completely nude but act very natural, as if they are dressed. There will be an intimate celebration where someone previously (by mutual agreement) selected will read and have the couple sign a marriage contract with drops of blood drawn from the ring fingers. (The marriage contract is shown at the end of this chapter.)

3. Struggle for Satisfaction

Both believe that if there is no merger, there is no love, "I want us to turn into only one being." Their mothers did not nurse them long enough. This has left them with the urge to suck milk to satiate themselves. They are pseudo adults who seek to be taken care of materially and emotionally: "Be in charge of me! Defend me against pain and suffering. Worry yourself with my health and comfort." Actually, they do not want to make a partnership with a man or a woman but with a mother or a father. The outcome is another frustrated baby who wants to cover up his weaknesses, passing himself off as a fulfilled man. "I have no need to nurse. To prove this, I am going to sacrifice myself for you. I am going to turn myself into your ideal mother-father. I will give you everything you want, but on the condition that you believe me. I will protect you and take care of you, even more so when you act like an adult—at which time I will become deeply depressed because I will have lost my function. I feel alive only if I worry about you. Never change!" Conflict occurs when whoever had the child's role begins to exercise the role of the mother-father. The dethroned other will grow weak and sick or will suffer from a serious accident or financial ruin. As one grows, the other retreats.

These people are bottomless pits. Their requests have no end. And becoming increasingly demanding proves that the other is incapable of satisfying. Unable to meet the demands, the other suffers: "Actually, I don't want to be loved, I want thanks!" The one who incessantly asks is, however, unable to be satisfied and is never thankful. For the consultants caught in this struggle, I recommend:

- **Monday:** Throughout the day, she will have her right eye bandaged, the right ear plugged, the right arm immobilized, and the right leg solidly bound to her partner's left leg. He will have his left eye bandaged, the left ear plugged, the left arm immobilized, and the left leg solidly bound to his partner's right leg. In this way, they will have to fiddle around to wash up, to cook, to eat, to run errands, and to work. The couple will sleep tied together, too.

- **Tuesday:** Always with the same ear plugged, she can only go from one place to the other—in the home or in public—by way of riding her partner's back. At night, they make love—him on her—she remains motionless as if dead.

- **Wednesday:** Always with the same sense deprivation in the same eye and ear, he can only go from one place to the other—in the home or in public—by way of riding his partner's back. At night, they make love—her on him—he remains motionless as if dead.

- **Thursday:** They take three baths together at 6 a.m., 6 p.m., and midnight. They repeat the following, three times during each bath: standing in the bathtub, they pour five gallons of milk over each other's heads. They put the thirty empty bottles in a bag and, dressed as babies, bury the bottles before dawn, planting thirty lilies over them.

- **Friday:** No one speaks all day. Time and meals are shared in silence. At night, the couple undress and lie alongside one another in bed, caressing. He penetrates her. United intimately like that, no one moves. Together and by memory, the couple recites the following text: "I accept what you are. Your words are my words, your love is my love, your desires are my desires, your life is my life. If you are not in me, I am a pebble on the path. Everything of mine is a river that is gliding toward your infinite sea. I have looked for you ever since I was born: you were the future that slept in the depths of my soul. Now, having found you, I have found myself. I know that when I think, you think of me; when I feel, you are the feeling; when I desire, it is because you desire. I only live when you live in me."

- **Saturday:** They invite relatives and friends to celebrate their marriage (or a new marriage if they are already married). Completely nude, they greet the guests, bound by handcuffs at the wrists, but act naturally, as if dressed. There will be an intimate ceremony at which someone previously chosen in mutual agreement will read aloud the marriage contract, which both sign with drops of blood drawn from their ring fingers. (The marriage contract is shown at the end of this chapter.)

4. Struggle for Power

Who dominates is the one who occupies 90 percent of this relationship. Each person, when young, did not have the opportunity to be him- or herself but was obligated to be what the dominating parents wanted him or her to be. These people grow up with an enormous desire to lord over someone else. If this is achieved, however, they lose interest in the relationship and run off.

The person who requires submission says, "I would like to submit and let you drive for me, without any resistance. You give the orders; you decide, like my parents did. But I can't. Nor do I want to. I am certain that if I do, then you will disregard me. Therefore, even though I enrage you, I will insist on asserting my independence. Sometimes I will threaten suicide so that you will understand that you should free me. However, in spite of all your insults, I don't want to separate from you. I am playing a cruel game that I myself made."

Whoever remains trapped and subdued by the other says, "Being a couple, one of the two must submit, and I assume the role because, during my childhood, I had to lower my head. With my parents, I could never have an opinion or satisfy my desires, nor could I disobey. Now that I have found you, weak, coward, I will take advantage of the situation and treat you exactly the way they treated me."

This "weak" person is inhabited by an enormous drive to master someone someday. On the other hand, the one who leads is insecure and only dominates because doing so demonstrates to himself that he is strong. When the dominated frees herself little by little (out of a fear of separation), concessions are launched and the roles reverse. For the consultants caught in this struggle, I recommend:

- **Monday:** Throughout the day, he, with a sign hanging from his neck that says "Master," gives his lover orders: reasonable, absurd, or odious. She, with a sign hanging from her neck that says "Slave," obeys without protest. At night, he has sex the way he wants it.
- **Tuesday:** Throughout the day, she, with a sign hanging from her neck that says "Master," gives her lover orders: reasonable, absurd, or odious. He, with a sign hanging from his neck that says "Slave," obeys without protest. At night, she has sex the way she wants it.
- **Wednesday:** They go out walking together, choosing very busy streets. He goes in a wheelchair, which she pushes. Contemptuously, insulting her, he shouts orders at her, and she, without a word, obeys.
- **Thursday:** They go out walking together, choosing very busy streets. She goes in a wheelchair, which he pushes. Contemptuously, insulting him, she shouts orders at him, and he, without a word, obeys.
- **Friday:** No one speaks all day. Time and meals are shared in silence. At night, they undress and caress one another. Standing in front of a full-length mirror, he penetrates her. Intimately connected this way, they don't move. Uniting their voices, they recite together by memory the following text: "Everything goes along: birthing, dying, transforming. We are never in the same place; we are never the same. We found, in the fleeting, a permanent union, moderating our desires in favor of health. Eliminating fleeting things of little value, we have achieved freedom. Ceasing to

identify ourselves with our personas, so that nothing can separate us from the creative energy, we have achieved union. We will die in one another, and we will return, transfigured. We will not have barriers between the human and the divine. We will be as much of what we are as of what we are not."

- **Saturday:** They invite relatives and friends to celebrate their marriage (or a new marriage if they are already married). Completely nude, they greet the guests, bound by handcuffs at the wrists, but act naturally, as if dressed. There will be an intimate ceremony at which someone previously chosen in mutual agreement will read aloud the marriage contract, which they sign with drops of blood drawn from their ring fingers.

The Marriage Contract

We have constructed an adult relationship, we are an adult couple, and we are balanced. Even though we profess opposite ideas and beliefs, we understand the value of respect. We have developed and continue to develop a benevolent comprehension that we have come to understand in silence. Under the pretext of the word love, we will never demand of the other the total gift of his or her self, trying to turn the other into food that fills our existential void. Eliminating childish desires for fusion, we will not force obstacles into the heart of the other so he or she will be able to develop all kinds of possibilities for love: love for him- or herself, for his or her relatives, for friends, and for all of humanity; for the planet, the universe; for the divine energy nesting in matter. We will free ourselves from all inhibition or exacerbation of our desires. We will experience pleasure, freeing it from possession. We will develop complicity and collaboration, allowing ourselves to explore one another. Economically independent, we will share work and space while conserving our private space and time. In case of need, we help one another, having learned the value of loyalty.

78. INCOMPREHENSIBLE WEEPING

There are people who, within the limits of our world, want for nothing. They have good relationships, health, money, but, without knowing why, sometimes they get sad and they cry. The brain, in tender childhood, may act as an emotional mirror: it copies the mother's feelings and, some time later, the father's and the grandparents' or those of whatever other relative. These feelings get stuck in the bottom of the memory and tend to, every so often, resurge. This incomprehensible sadness is not ours, and we can, in a symbolic way, return it to its owner.

- The consultant takes any object, concentrates on it, wets it with her tears (if she can't cry, she wets it with her saliva), and sends it to the relative whose problem she has reflected in a gift box, accompanied by a card that says, "This belongs to you. It is not mine." In cases where she cannot discover to whom this invading sadness belongs, while she cries or while she is depressed, it is comforting to suck a bottle full of sweet milk.

79. UNPROVOKED DEPRESSION, CONTINUOUS ANGUISH, AND BIRTH MASSAGE

At the beginning of a pregnancy, life arrives like an explosion of happiness. If the parents have not developed a high level of consciousness, their spiritual limitations and their physical imperfections will mix sinister pain with a sublime happiness. The embryo, from the first hours of its creation, absorbing what constitutes its environment (contributions that are not only material but also psychic), makes the traumas of the parents its own.

When, for different motives, the pregnant woman does not want to be a mother and fruitlessly tries to eliminate the fetus during all the months of gestation because she feels invaded by it, or she hopes to lose it, or she hopes the baby is born dead, then she will experience an anguished rejection during childbirth. Meanwhile, the unborn being will have the orders not to exist, not to be born but to die, to disappear, recorded in its cells. Most births come painfully (premature, overdue, suffocating, strangling, crossways), and the being then grows up without knowing what it is to be awaited with love or joyfully delivered. The mother's desire to eliminate the child turns into orders. The child's unconscious causes him or her to endlessly feel, "You have no right to exist. You do not exist. You should disappear." The child's harrowing experience with gestation, birth, and nursing projects an inexplicable suffering into daily life.

Whoever was born with forceps will live fighting against immense obstacles. Each fulfillment will cost him such stifling wastes of energy that it will seem impossible to even help himself so he will endlessly implore the help of others: help that, once obtained, will cause intense discomfort.

Birth by cesarean is disappointing for the child. She will not receive the loving final caresses of the vagina, she will not have come to life via her desire to be born and the mother's desire to give birth, but rather she is extracted as if she is a tumor. Later, for lack of confidence, she will live without the power to find the affection she seeks. She gets ready to obtain favorable results, but after her efforts, she will feel deprived of her rights and suffer from continuous disappointments. She will need to return to the starting point because she feels that there is something that remains incomplete.

The fetus who, being a victim of the problems of his mother wanting to keep him prisoner forever in her womb, could not adopt a good position for birth and was born breech or feet first, will, later in life, as an adult, live disoriented with the continuous feeling of regression, locating his goals in retrospect, sinking more and more into the family trap. He will search with desperation for individuals with strong personalities who will give him the missing plan that he needs to fulfill his desires.

The child who was born premature, still not ready to leave the uterus, feels ejected. The conflicts of her parents have turned her body into a battleground. Her birth will reveal the harmful family relationships. The woman, from the beginning, did not want to be pregnant by the man; she has conceived in disgust, hoping for a spontaneous abortion. As this did not happen, she wants to get rid of the fetus as quickly as possible. The child grows up sad, plunged in a state of emotional poverty.

If a child is born overdue (can sometimes be after ten months) because of emotional and physical traumas, the amniotic liquid will be consumed and the dryness and heat of the uterus will dry the baby's skin. On the other hand, the supplementary weeks of gestation will have increased the volume of the baby's head, which makes the birth more difficult, like hitting a wall. The adult who suffered this kind of birth will constantly feel threatened, the prisoner of relationships that have no solution. He probably has chosen a very difficult way to live, never staying in one place. He will accuse his partners in emotional relationships of not helping and of impeding his fulfillment.

There are many way in which the difficult birth appears. Generally, the child is accused of causing these difficulties: "You wrapped yourself around the umbilical chord; you grew too much; you turned; you didn't want to come out; you decided to be born after your time." Actually, when the mother is altered by family problems, which have traumatized her since her own birth, it is she herself who causes the child's agitation or passivity. She should say, "I wrapped the cord around your neck because I wanted to eliminate you; I made you grow too much so you wouldn't come out because I was afraid of being a mother; I turned you around so that you would always be mine and you would come toward me, not toward the world; I retained you longer than nine months because I was afraid of not knowing how to take care of you; I ejected you before your time because I was not sure of being the mother you needed, nor was I sure of my selection for the man who inseminated me."

Born stunned by sedatives or nearly asphyxiated or very sore due to hours of efforts, people who suffered these difficulties will feel that they lack maternal love, and they will continuously seek it for most of their lives. The future is loaded with menacing threats because the future (during birth) was agony. These adults will deposit their hopes for fulfillment into the hands of others, trying secretly to play the role of the victim. Everything will happen for reasons independent of their own will. They struggled hard in order to emerge from the maternal sex. They arrange their lives so that everything in their lives becomes a struggle: they will invent their difficulties; many will cling to a small territory (very small rooms), where they feel that the smallness will protect them from the ravages of life. Very few things can satisfy them; they feel frustrated, ugly, bad, useless, incapable, unloved. They feel like it doesn't matter to the world if they are alive or dead. Suddenly, full of impulsivity, they will make desperate attempts—the same ones they made in order to come out of the uterus—submerging themselves in incessant activities. They wear themselves out working, without being able to free themselves of the feeling of catastrophic loneliness. Feeling cruelly abandoned, they search for someone to help them, demanding foolish relief without ever thinking that they themselves can help themselves. Picky and, at the same time, ungrateful, they will have lost the capacity to trust. They won't believe in anything or even in themselves.

The more one tells the consultant born in one of these ways that happiness resides in herself, the more she cannot find it because she lacks the needed information, which is a sum of nonverbal actions and experiences. For the consultant to obtain this freeing information, it is necessary for her to receive a birth massage (a psychomagic ceremony where words, employed as charms at the service of gestures, supply the consultant with information nature had programmed during normal gestation, birth, and nursing). It is necessary for this ceremony to be conducted by therapists (a man and a woman): the word *therapist,* in accordance with its Greek etymology, meaning "service: take care of something or someone," designates charitable people who have the same culture (ethnicity, socioeconomic class) as the consultant, and who put themselves at the service of a human being, knowing that to heal any other is also to cure oneself.

- ▶ Whoever acts the role of the parents should meet privately, before working with the consultant. They will have had a bath previously in order to eliminate natural odors and perfumes. They will also take care to not eat food that gives them gas because any strong odor might distract the consultant, diverting him toward projections that will impede a satisfactory contact with the therapists: the organs of the feelings transmit subliminal information to the brain, we see more than what we believe we see, we smell more than what we believe we smell, we hear more than what we believe we hear. A color, an odor, a shape, a sound can awaken in our minds memories, messages, correlations, events with huge magnitude. For this same reason, the therapists should not adorn themselves (rings, watches, pendants, broaches). It is necessary also that they don't wear clothes that can identify them with a style, time period, or an economic situation: good or bad.

Preferentially, the man should wear a shirt and white pants, and the woman should wear a large, one-piece, simple black dress. These clothes will have been washed before the ceremony so that they are not impregnated with strong odor. He and she should hug and put their torsos together for quite a while, feeling the beating of the heart of the other and controlling the respiration until both acquire the same rhythm. They then begin to adapt their voices, eliminating nasal or guttural echos, each pronouncing the syllable *a* and the other syllable *mour* (*amour,* the French word for love), so that, with total calmness and taking as a base the zone of the chest, they get to an agreeable tone, the same that is used to calm down a small child.

The place where the massage will be given (into which one should enter barefoot) should be a clean room with as little furniture as possible and without any adornments or paintings on the walls: nothing to distract the consultant's attention from himself. Prepared in this way, the couple calls the consultant. The consultant takes the male therapist's hands and says, "During the duration of the ceremony, I accept that you represent [first and last names], my father." The therapist responds, with the same intonation used with a child in order not to scare the child, "During the duration of this ceremony, I will be your father." The consultant takes the female therapist's hands and tells her, "During the duration of this ceremony, I accept that you represent [first and last names], my mother." The therapist responds, "During the duration of this ceremony, I will be your mother."

Standing in front of the consultant—each with a cushion at his or her feet so the consultant can punch it when pent-up rage surges—the therapists ask the consultant to tell them everything the consultant has against them, expressing his rage, shame, disgust, hate, need to be loved. When the consultant realizes that these complaints are not sufficient to repair the emotional havoc, he condemns the parents to death. It is important for the consultant to not mimic killing his parents by shotgun or ax, but rather, with absolute authority, the consultant orders it, "As they were, they do not deserve to live in my memory! Let them die!"

Pronouncing these words, the therapists fall down, lying on the floor, on their backs with their eyes closed. The consultant, on his knees before them, should express what he feels (the emotion). When the therapists infer that it has been expressed, they should say these words to the consultant, in a serious, slow, and friendly voice, "The evil we did to you was involuntary, caused by the evil that they did to us. If you have been able to eliminate us, it is because in you there is a strength capable of surpassing the obstacles that impede your arriving to yourself. Upon killing us, your old individuality, a deforming mold, which we imposed on you, has also begun to die. You will stop being who you believe you are and turn into who you truly are. We gave you the little bit we could give you. In spite of our defects, you were born, thanks to us; thanks to the suffering we put before you, you are stronger, and you have arrived at this moment of freedom. Commit an act of supreme value: forgive us. Without this forgiveness, you will never be capable of abandoning your child decoy.

"Recognize in your heart the immensity of your love. The hate that you had was only love that you believed was not reciprocated. But we, like you, because of our parents and grandparents, protected ourselves emotionally without being capable of transmitting love and consciousness. And this causes suffering: suffering that has plagued many generations. The same way that we are now doing this with you, besides forgiving ourselves, we have compassion for ourselves. To be deprived of the love of our children is a deep suffering. Also, understand that the pain that attracts the family makes you realize that, even though you are very right, not being like we want you to be shows us our limitations and our lack of awareness. We react with pain, anger, and disenchantment for not seeing that we were like a pressure cooker—full of ideas, feelings, desires, and inhibited needs. Because of this suffering that you caused us, if you take pity on our frustrated life, you will also be able to ask us for forgiveness." When the consultant is able to say, "I forgive you," followed by, "Forgive me," the therapists will recommend, "Let us rebirth now just like you wanted us to be."

The consultant should help the therapists to their feet, beginning with either the father or mother, then tell each how to positively parent. Each consultant will describe the ideal parents differently. What follows are two examples of the ideal father and the ideal mother.

For example, for the father, "You, my dear father, were present during my childhood giving me the feeling of safety, you worried about my development, turning me into an ally of my tastes and dreams, communicating the hope that my life will end sublimely. I want to see you in peace with yourself, with a mind opened to new knowledge and facing obstacles bravely, while encouraging me to conquer my values and supporting me when I feel weak, allowing me to act with freedom when I feel able. I want you to be attentive and proud of my progress. I don't want you to promise me stuff you can't give me. I want you to help me overcome fear. I want you to be just but not authoritative. I want you to take me in your tender arms, to put in the work to teach me what you know, to not force me to do something or force me into blind obedience but to, with love, persuade me. Allow me to soak you up without conflict, without your feeling robbed, helping me to identify with the best parts of you, transmitting your level of consciousness, allowing me to go further than you. Ideally, with happiness, let me supercede you. But, above all, I want you to love yourself so you can love me."

For example, for the mother, "My dear mother, I want you,

above all, besides loving me with your whole soul, to not be a domestic prostitute living your chores as if a victim. I want your tenderness to be infused in joy, such that the care you give me is not an oppressive obligation you do without pleasure. I want your caresses to not be possessive. I want what you say about life not to be hot air but the fruit of your vital experiences. I want you to be present in each important moment of my life, giving me your unconditional support. I want you to not criticize me negatively but by making me conscious of my errors, show me the correct paths, paths which you have traveled. I want you to love me without considering me to be one of your organs or your viscera. I want you to lock yourself in yourself; I don't want you to see me as a mirror at your service. I want you to listen to me, with your attention, tolerating that I don't always think as you do. I want you to realize that the world that you conceive can be different than what I conceive. I want you to be my accomplice, to support me even if you think I am wrong, to let me live my experiences even though they are errors. I want you to trust in me and, apart from your love, offer me your friendship and quit keeping what grieves you a secret. I want you to understand that, at birth, I quit being yours. I will always be with you, materially and spiritually, but I belong to myself."

Now the therapists, face-to-face, ask the consultant to tell them how he wants to see them in union. This can be, among other things, "I want to see your bodies united with pleasure and delicacy. I want you to give kisses that are rooted in your souls. I want to feel that you are ready to support one another in adversity and to celebrate together the good events. I want to see tolerance in your minds. I want to see you free to think and to believe what you want without entering into conflict because the other thinks or believes differently. From these different thoughts and beliefs, I want you to do everything complementarily. I don't want to witness a debate that is devoid of a conversation but rather an agreement made on a mutual goal and with a love that guides your differences. I want your hearts to vibrate with happiness, celebrating the other's existence, desiring to give without asking, to receive and accept what is given when it is offered of one's own volition. I want you to desire one another naturally without inhibiting or forcing attraction, accepting these desires as a divine drive. I want you, father, to be for mother a lover, a father, a friend, a son, a sage. I want you, mother, to be for father a lover, a mother, a friend, a daughter, a sage."

When the consultant has described the perfect parental union, the therapists will say, "You have arrived at the moment when you give yourself life. What posture do you want to adopt to beget yourself?" Then the consultant will choose the desired posture, such as lying beneath the mother and the father on top or vice versa or standing up. The therapists, avoiding any pornographic aspect, with elegance and delicacy, will mimic, in the requested posture, a mutual orgasm full of happiness. Then the therapists will tell the consultant, "You have witnessed your conception. You have been conceived with pleasure." The therapist will add, "Now, with pleasure, you will install yourself in your mother's belly."

The consultant is completely nude. The therapists begin to give him an energetic massage, by securing the feeling of a formless body. Little by little, they put the consultant in the fetal position as they murmur, "Within you, there is no ego or form or name or sex. Offering your life will end your identity and you will disappear. You are pure material, fruit of universal consciousness." Then they attach a cord to the waist to symbolize the umbilical cord. The consultant can choose the material: a silk ribbon, a red rope, a plastic tube, or a chain. (If he opts for the last one, he must also foresee an instrument capable of cutting it.)

The female therapist undresses. The male therapist takes care of the consultant, placing him on the female therapist's belly and then ties the other end of the cord to the "mother" and covers them with a soft and warm fabric. From this moment on, the therapists, while caressing the bulging shape that is the consultant beneath the fabric (as if it were the full belly of a pregnant mother), describe the stages of his development month by month, speaking with a loving voice and slowly to allow the "child" to incorporate the concepts and allow him to sit in the mind and body like in a deep meditation.

First Month

Him: First month.

Her: How wonderful! We are going to have a child like we have always wanted!

These words, simple but essential, should be pronounced with a tone that expresses the joy of begetting the consultant just as he is. A large number of people live devaluing themselves because their parents wanted a boy but a girl was born, or vice versa.

Him: It appears that you are only a little bit of matter, but just like inside of a tiny seed is a big tree, the same force capable of generating the galaxy vibrates within you.

Her: Feel the creative power that animates in you, and give yourself over to the jubilant ecstasy that is the essence of matter. Attend these sacred moments in what the universal consciousness transforms in your flesh. Consciousness and flesh are one and the same thing: there is no separation between you and the substance of the cosmos. As you nourish yourself from me, you are fortifying me. You give health to my viscera; you purify my blood; you clean my spirit of old suffering; you extract me from the past; you submerge me in the present.

Him: You free me from the fear of loss; you infuse me with value. You inoculate me with the necessary strength to face the future. You give me the security I need to convince myself that I will always be able to protect you: you and your mother. As you grow, you build us.

Second Month

Him: Second month.

Her: Feel how, in this material that you are and which duplicates itself over and over again with the desire to fill the world, a heartbeat is born and comes from the greatest depth of the universe. Your center has appeared around which your heart is forming, the fountain from which divine loves pours. All of life is beating around you. Now, you are no longer a formless mass. With a healthy appetite, absorb the pure nourishment I give to you, full of hope that it will create healthy blood, balanced organs, vigorous viscera, and conscious systems.

Him: Grow up without apprehension, trust in us, dear child of mine: we have purified ourselves to give you the best of our bodies and souls.

Third Month

Her: Third month.

Him: Your androgynous energy divides. Now you know if you are man or woman. We accept the sex which you have chosen to incarnate. You obey the universal forces that know what they are doing. This definition is the root of your identity.

Her: Through me, you begin to communicate with the world. You receive the exterior as I receive it. Through your blood, your veins, your arteries, you ascend the umbilical cord and enter into my mind.

Him: Knowing you are vulnerable to what the body feels and that the body contains and nourishes you, this is why I protect your mother, providing her with calm and tranquility, keeping her away from negative emotions, because I want the world that you find in her mind to not contain elements that cause you anguish.

Her: My child, your pure soul, upon entering mine, my illnesses are healed, my metabolism is balanced. The suffering I had before your arrival has transformed into fertile land, which you have given significance. Grow! When you are born, no matter what state the world is in, you will be a carrier of peace and happiness for all of us.

Fourth Month

Her: Fourth month.

Him: Your mass increases. Your whole body soaks up the divine energy. Your head's mass has decreased, your limbs grow; you are conscious of yourself, of your sacred shape, of the perfect balance between what you feel you are and what you actually are.

Her: Your bones are solidifying. Feeling the skeleton in your flesh flourish, I understand that you prepare to support yourself, to walk your own path. I know perfectly that I am not creating you but that I am receiving you. In this way, full of love for you, I give each cell of my body the chance to evolve without obstacles.

Fifth Month

Her: Fifth month.

Him: The velocity of your growth has decreased. You employ the best part of your energy in feeling yourself; you know the happiness that dwells in the bone marrow. With the small and delightful movements of your limbs, you announce to your mother that you are alive: that you are you, not her.

Her: You have freed yourself from my mind. You are developing your own feelings. You hear the sounds that cross the flesh of the belly you are nesting in. It is the world that waits for you, telling you that your birth will mean the beginning of a marvelous change. And in this joining of rhythms and sounds—each with its own life, with energy that nurtures you as much as the blood you receive from me—they carry to you our voices, mine and your father's, intertwined with love.

Her and Him: You will never hear us argue or fight or take on aggressive tones that are not harmonious. Our voices, united like two hands that pray, bless you now and forever.

Him: Although without seeing, you open your eyes, because your ancestral memory tells you of the existence of light. You know that the darkness in which you float is divine emptiness that begot you, and with it as an ally, you will move toward the light that calls you toward the exterior. This light is the essence of your matter: you are a being of light.

Her: Your nose has also formed. You already sense the nostalgia of oxygen's pure aroma in your nose. If I give you matter, it is your father who offers you air. When you breathe outside, you will inhale the breath of the unimaginable God. The divine breath that unites us and turns you, us, all of humanity, all living beings, into one lung, into one consciousness.

Him: If, with the nose, you perceive the depth of the cosmos, in your tongue you impatiently wait all the tastes of Earth—salty, sweet, bitter, acidic—but above all, the sublime taste of water, a charitable liquid that will reveal to you the transparency of your soul, the adaptability of your mind to innumerable shapes, the pacifist's strength of penetration, which is love, where everything dissolves into a vivacious ecstasy.

Her: Your hands learn to open and close: that is to say, to receive, and to give. Touching, they are harmoniously shaping the brain so that, upon taking possession of yourself, your feelings open just like flowers in the spring before winter.

Sixth Month

Her: Sixth month.

Him (if the consultant is a woman): You are already shaped as a person. The androgynous original has turned into a woman. Your vagina, your uterus, your ovaries have developed. Concentrating, you feel in your sex where eternity lives. You are the carrier of millions of eggs. You are not only shaping yourself but you are also shaping the humanity to come. My daughter, your sex is a temple, a link in the sacred chain that is born in the divine consciousness.

Her (if the consultant is a man): You are already shaped like a person. The androgynous original has turned into a man. Your penis and your testicles have developed. Concentrating, you feel in your sex where eternity lives. Sperm is made in your gonads. They are not permanent like the female eggs that last a life time; they are ephemeral and constantly multiply. Life is the encounter between the eternal and the fleeting. You are not only shaping yourself, but you are also shaping the humanity to come. My son, your sex is a temple, a link in the sacred chain that is born in the divine consciousness.

Him: And your brain is also a temple: you have received, as an inheritance, absolute memory; your neurons contain dreams and illusions of your billions of ancestors . . .

Her: . . . and even now, you carry stamps of all of your future projects: the moment at which you mutate, creating a new brain; the moment at which you develop telepathy; the moment at which, through your mental strength, you can levitate; the moment of the great emigration to a new galaxy; the moment at which you will populate the whole universe. Already, all of this is within you, my darling child.

Seventh Month

Him: Seventh month.

Her: Your skin, your whole being, layer by layer, has thickened; through it, you are united with the totality. It is not a surface separating you from the world but an open frontier: feel your innumerable pores, through them you give and receive. You breathe in the divine consciousness; you absorb it, you digest it, you pass away through your whole body: you are a sacred being.

Him: In the fingerprints of your fingers, in the palms of your hands, and in the soles of your feet, lines have formed that are different from those of the rest of the human beings; these prove that you are unique, that you come to carry the world something that only you possess: your precious identity. No one has ever been nor will ever be you; you will be enrolled in eternity like a precious and unique jewel.

Her: Your face has now formed. It is a window through which the interior and exterior communicate with and join one another. The past is spread out behind your face; the future extends out in front of your face. In your features the present is reflected, which is nothing other than your soul.

Him: In order to come to the world just as you are and not like others wanted you to be, you need to communicate with me. If, by the umbilical cord, you are attached to your mother, the cord that attaches me to you is my voice. Tell me, knowing that I am an aspect of you yourself, what it is that you want me to tell you so that you can complete your development in good shape. Ask me, demand me: I am listening to you with the whole of my being.

The consultant asks the "father" what he would have wanted the father to say at the moment he was made. The therapist should repeat with a sweet and deep voice exactly, phrase by phrase, what the consultant asks him to say.

Eighth Month

Her: Eighth month.

Him: In this infinite peace in which you developed, you do not know if you are dreaming awake or if you are asleep with your mother, both united in the same dream. Through your unconsciousness, you receive the wisdom of your ancestors, not in the shape of precise memories but as intense energy. And you, with your new cells, are capable of receiving the projects of the future. You are the avatar, the descent of a glorious being in a mortal body.

Her: Do not be afraid of this descent: in order to feel your divine nobility, you must pass painfully from small worldly organs to the huge cosmic organs. What, in the beginning, you confuse with pain are only the charitable contradictions that open the animal borders up and give you the sublime expansion of your consciousness. Feel the beat of your heart: in it, the center of the universe rests. Your brain prepares mutations that will make you our teacher.

Him: Your spirit incarnates in accordance with the universal plan; your body develops correctly. You sensitive zones appear. The sexual energy activates, the development of the nerves around your mouth preparing you to suck the nipples, sublime feeling that is summarized in only one phrase, the basis of your whole language: thank you. The emotional energy teaches you to swallow, the vital act that gives your spirit its essential activity: receive. The mental energy teaches you to yawn; you relax accepting the benefits of the past and the projects of the future, you learn "to trust." The material energy teaches you to attach so that you can explore with caution but without fear, your body, preparing you to investigate the exterior, the other, the world. In the opening and closing of the hands, you realize that everything you touch is only lent to you, including this body that is forming, to which one day you will quit going around with the same happiness you have today. Love it because it is the vehicle for your soul.

Her: Now that your hearing is formed, feel this music, absorb it, let it enter your heart, circling in the bloodstream.

The therapists have the consultant listen to soft, choral music in order to relax. For a few minutes, both caress the bundle formed by the consultant and impress delicate movements on the consultant to have him follow the musical rhythm.

Ninth Month

Her: Ninth month.

Him: You continue to grow, your space has reduced. You almost have no more space to move around: you cannot stretch out your arms or your legs; you feel uncomfortable, pained. However, a wave of warm, vital energy invades you. You feel the enjoyable stability of your digestive apparatus, healthily formed; you feel the potency of your lungs that are now completely ready to ingest the miraculous oxygen; you open, in the darkness, your eyes already capable of capturing the anxious light. This happiness that defeats the pain is summarized in a facial feature: a smile. Ascending movements in the corners of your lips remind you that in every moment your spirit is weightless; your consciousness, free from the weight of matter, can elevate and travel to the limits of the universe.

Her: Smile, because, the tightness in which you reside wraps you in a comfortable warmth. You are never hungry; you are protected from harsh sounds and harsh lights; my heartbeat is a constant sound that comforts you. All of this tells you, "You are you and I am me." From now on, you can be born; you have the right to be what you are: to feel, to see, to hear, to touch, to taste, to smell, without limitations, whatever your divine curiosity desires to know and experience. You have the right to think what you want, to love whom you want to love, to desire without imposing limitations on yourself, to fulfill that for which the universe created you.

Him: Keep in your spirit this continuous prayer: I am from you, I trust you, you are my happiness.

Her: When you feel ready, begin to turn until you've put your head facing downward. You will decide the moment of your birth. I will collaborate with you without any opinions about your designs. You will direct; I will follow you. Between the two of us, we will accomplish a joyous delivery.

Patiently, the therapists wait for the consultant to decide to be born. If he has absorbed the massage of the nine months, it will not take long to turn the head downward and start to emerge and enter the arms of the therapist who is facing the consultant, giving the sensation of emerging from the mother's sex. As the consultant mimics being born, the female therapist also imitates an intense orgasm.

Her: Stretch and fill my vagina. I give birth to you with absolute pleasure. My breasts swell and throb in pleasure.

Upon coming out completely from under the sheets, the consultant is received with tenderness by the male therapist, who takes him and puts him in the arms of the female therapist. The two therapists express a great happiness for having received such a beautiful child. The "mother," with scissors, cuts the umbilical cord.

Her: You are my child but you are also the child of the world. Upon cutting the cord, I grant you the totality of your life, of that which you are responsible. You have been born. In your memory, the memory of milk full of love is recorded.

The female therapist pours condensed milk on the nipples of one of her breasts and allows the consultant to suck, nursing. After finishing this rite, the male therapist asks, "What would you like to be named?" If the consultant, after analyzing his genealogy tree, has understood that the name that his parents gave him is charged with negative significance, the consultant should choose a new name. The therapists, finalizing the ceremony with the change of name, should wash the consultant, treating him as if he were a baby. They soap the consultant with much attention, dry him with tenderness, and help to dress him in new clothes. No old clothes should be kept, not even rings or watches. Once the consultant is dressed, the therapists each take him by the hand and go for a walk. The therapists walk with the consultant as if he were a child. The therapists may buy the consultant a pastry or a candy. Then they should part company with the consultant.

Her and Him: The ceremony of your second birth has ended. Let us stop personifying your parents. Do not follow us. Now you are your own father and your own mother. Stop asking. Invest, sow, develop your consciousness.

The consultant should go without looking back.

80. REMEDY FOR PESSIMISTS

To heal any illness, it is necessary to first want to heal. If the sick one does not want to be healed, the doctor can't heal. For a long time, I felt incapable of helping those who brag about not liking anything, claiming that the world deserves only to be spit upon. Suddenly, I found in *Gay Science,* a book by Friedrich Nietzsche, a poem in which the philosopher drained his patience and his heart by listening to pessimists complain, shout, and spit insults. He advised them to

- swallow a fat toad every morning

so that, for the rest of the day, they would not find anything disgusting. I think it is excellent psychomagic advice, which, of course, will not be accepted by those who need it. One thing is to give; another thing is to force someone to receive.

TWO

Psychomagic Recommendations for Society

Acts to Heal Communities, Countries, and the World

If psychomagic acts can heal the individual, it is possible and necessary to create acts that heal whole communities. This is difficult work because, to achieve this, one must reach different mentalities, many times antagonistic, and accept them willingly. Social psychomagic should remain apolitical, in no way sacrilegious or destructive. The acts need only to be beautiful in order to heal and expand consciousness. This sociopsychomagic activity should be supported by the governmental authorities. So until governments realize that the political-economical solutions, the colonialism, the revolutions, and the wars are not sufficient means to solve the self-destructive chaos into which humanity plunges more and more, it will have to be generous individuals, aware that a spiritual mutation is necessary, who organize collective acts to guide people to places of peace, harmony, and joy-filled living.

POLITICAL DISAPPEARANCES

A group of Chilean women asked me for an act so their souls could rest, distraught as they were over their relatives who had disappeared by force during the reign (1970–1980) of Augusto Pinochet (1915–2006). The members of this society did not have a corpse to grieve over or a grave at which to leave flowers. I recommended:

- Go to a desert (if not possible, go to a wasteland) and dig holes as deep as possible. At the bottom of each hole, put in a cage, each with a dove that clutches in its claw a small piece of rolled-up parchment paper on which is written the word *freedom*. Kneel down together around the holes and cry as much as possible for the disappeared. Some relatives go to the bottoms of the holes and open the cages to let the doves escape. Refill the pits by putting quartz crystal rocks in the cages.

THE NIGHT OF TLATELOLCO

The director general of the Centro Cultural Universitario de Tlatelolco (CCUT) asked me for a cleansing act for the killings of a hundred students, which was committed by the military in the plaza of this residential neighborhood in Mexico City in 1968. The memory of these murders haunted the inhabitants of this cluster of tall buildings. I sent the following proposal:

- A hundred sets of mariachis surround this poisoned plaza and play, in unison, the song "La Llorona." (La Llorona [the weeping woman] is a poor woman who killed her children. Turned into a wandering ghost, she laments them.) During this musical overture, several men dressed in black and wearing skull masks on their faces spread, over the whole surface of the plaza, a tapestry filled with tiny, red plastic balls. This tapestry symbolizes splattered blood.

Upon transforming the plaza into a big rectangular arena, an orchestra plays (live, if possible, otherwise recorded) a sublime symphony of Mexican music. Together with this symphony, large groups of male and female students from ages seven to nine sweep up the plastic balls with brooms, beginning at one side of the plaza and ending at the other side, where there will be a large transparent, plastic bag in the form of a human being with its arms opened like a cross. Other children fill this form with the tiny balls until it has turned into an enormous red man lying in the plaza. At least two thousand, or as many as are needed, white balloons filled with helium are tied to the red man until it is lifted and carried to the sky. Then five hundred women enter wearing long white skirts, their torsos naked, and carrying babies, also naked, in their arms. They sit in the now cleaned plaza nursing their babies. Three military helicopters arrive and spray a shower of white bookmarks with poems printed on them: pre-Columbian poems and poems by Mexican poets of different time periods that exalt life. When this white rain has ceased, the helicopters leave, and a plane arrives to write in the sky with smoke the word *hope*, as the neighbors hang green flags in all the windows of the buildings.

(The director told me there were not enough funds to organize such an act.)

A HARBOR FOR BOLIVIA

It is regrettable that Bolivia does not have a door to the ocean. In a private interview with President Michele Bachelet (president of Chile, 2006–2010),

- I proposed that Chile give a harbor to Bolivia without asking anything from it in exchange. With this selfless act, Chile could be a great example to all countries in the world, teaching them how to collaborate instead of compete.

FEMALE POPES IN ROME

- Because the ecclesiastic authority is invested in a solitary man (representing God the Father, excluding Goddess the Mother), I recommend, in order to protest as pacifists, that a thousand or more women, dressed as female popes, show up to receive blessings from the pope when he makes a public appearance at the Vatican.

RALLY FOR PEACE

- On a main street in a city in the United States, organize a protest in which only the mothers of the white and black races participate. Open an exchange of babies. The white women carry black babies in their arms, and the black women carry white babies in their arms, and, if necessary, the women nurse the babies they carry. The women organize themselves in two long, parallel lines. A line of black and white men walk between the two lines of women; the men carry posters that simply read "Peace": some written in black letters on a white background, others written in white letters on a black background.

PROTEST AGAINST HUNGER

- In any commercial center in any developed country, organize a silent protest whose participants are exclusively very fat men and woman who each carry a photograph of an extremely malnourished child.

HOSTILE WALLS

- On each side of the long walls that separate Mexico and the United States or Israel and Palestine, very good artists from around the whole world paint large doors of all styles to give passage freely to wide open spaces and beautiful landscapes, skies, cities.

COLLECTIVE HEALING

The herd instinct makes it essential for the individual to be recognized and integrated into society. It takes longer for an isolated sick person to heal than it does for someone who receives affection from a collective. Among the 613 commandments of the Hebrew religion, the most important is to go visit the ill. People of goodwill should meet together to bring about collective healing. In December of 2007, I put into practice a social psychomagic act at the Teatro Caupolicán in Santiago, Chile. I asked the six thousand people who attended, sitting in a circle surrounding the rectangular stage, to concentrate only on thinking of curing someone. I made a forty-year-old woman stop in the middle of the stage. For twenty years she had difficulty talking due to a surgery and thyroid cancer. Her voice was like a high-pitched wire, barely comprehendible. It was enough to say, "We are all healers," because all six thousand people extended their hands toward the woman sending her the energy they wished to be healing. The woman, crying with emotion, received this emotional impact. For a few minutes, she was the center of the world: she was surrounded by a human mass, wishing healing for her. We knew her family had forced her to marry a man she did not love. The cancer began with the birth of her daughter—now a twenty-year-old woman—who never heard her mother's normal voice. Within a few minutes, the woman felt something open in her throat. Months later, her voice had recovered as well as a happiness to be alive. She began to take voice lessons. Her relationship with her daughter got notably better.

For collective healing, I recommend:

- Gather together a group of as many individuals as possible and, seated in a circle, guide the palms of their hands toward the sick person, wishing him or her to be healed. Each session can be to give beneficial treatment to as many sick people as needed, and five to eight minutes is sufficient for the patient to receive the energy of this amorous attention, like a precious gift that the collective lavishes on the patient. While the "healers" send their "waves," the men should murmur the syllable *a* and the women the syllable *mour* (*amour,* the French word for love).

ANTI–OLYMPIC GAMES

The Olympic Games are organized like a war: each nation intends to master the others, and the winners feel proud and superior while the losers are sad and humiliated. I pray for the day when a government understands that the Olympic Games should focus on the goal of triumph for the human race and not a triumph for a nation. If an athlete, for example, beats a record, and he or she becomes the fastest runner in history, this is not an exploit that should be celebrated only in the runner's birth country but on the whole planet. Athletes don't need to have a nationality.

- In a conscious country, I propose to create an Anti–Olympics Games, in which human beings from all corners of the planet come together with the intention of awarding triumphs to the whole of humanity. In these games, there are no flags or regional uniforms or national hymns. The prizes, simple crowns of laurel leaves, will be given to the athletes by boys and girls of all races, without identification with a nation.

WORLD UNION

▶ Through the Internet, the majority of inhabitants on the planet should agree to paint (from the main street of the capital of a randomly chosen country), with permanent purple paint, a seven-inch-wide line. This line—added to in length by people of goodwill who desire world union—should circle the world. The government of every nation should offer the paint for free. At the small stretches of water, the line may circle it; in the case of rivers, the line can go over the bridge. The line, in a symbolic way, painted on three-foot-long pieces of wood, can cross the oceans and be continued on the other side.

THREE

Psychomagic Acts for Maintaining Health

Dancing the Cosmic Dance

Although it appears that we have accomplished living with equality and security, the territory that we have conquered, which we feel unalterable, belongs to a world of continuous change and expansion. We do not live enclosed in a house, on a street, in a city, in a country: we evolve on a planet that participates in a cosmic dance. It carries us through space around the sun at 19 miles per second. The solar system is traveling around the center of the galaxy at 143 miles per second. The Milky Way Galaxy travels toward its neighbor, the Andromeda Galaxy, at 56 miles per second. The group composed of the Milky Way and the Andromeda Galaxies travels at 37 miles per second, attracted by the Virgo Supercluster and the Hydra and Centaurus Superclusters, which travel toward another huge agglomeration of tens of thousands of galaxies. And, little by little, we travel to the limits, where our universe is attracted by a universe even more complex and vast, which, in turn, rotates around another, forming a pluriverse.

In this immeasurable cosmic dance, everything is being born, dying, transforming. How then do we define this? To the extent that the individual evolves his or her consciousness, the links between the brain cells multiply. Accepting the unity of matter, we understand that all is related, and that the universe is a totality in which nothing acts separately. We can conceive that this mysterious energy that unites the neurons is also capable of uniting brains. We can call these collective unions *egregores* (from the Greek word *egregoroi*). The French occult magician and poet, Eliphas Levi (Alphonse Louis Constant, 1810–1875), defines them as "spirits of energy and action, princes of the soul." We will have a familial egregore, a national egregore (symbolized by the animals: Russian bear, North American eagle, French rooster, Spanish bull, Chilean deer) and a planetary egregore created by all of humanity. The individual is ephemeral; the human race can be immortal. In order to go from "self" to "us" and to participate in the cosmic project, the universe in evolution, where each atom will be a spirit, we have to manage to detach from mental moorings so that nothing subjective separates us from the creative energy. We give up "belonging to," "identifying with," and "defining ourselves" in order to arrive at union. We are a chalice that has ideas, but we are not these ideas, just like we are not our feelings or desires. We should take these thoughts-feelings-desires (inculcated by our family, society, and culture) as raw material and submit them to a process to mutate them—a process in which we should die to ourselves and return to be born, transfigured, no longer being a body that encircles a spirit but a spirit that navigates from body to body until the ends of creation. We don't define ourselves as young or old, women or men, no diploma, no uniform, no name, no nationality to limit our impersonal endeavors. Under the individual mask, we enjoy the peace of anonymity; not having barriers between the human and the divine, we know the whole universe. We live many years like the universe; we turn into the consciousness of the universe; we create ourselves eternally. The fulfillment of the individual is impossible if this does not include the goal of comprising the whole human race.

Given the underdeveloped consciousness of our time, these aims can appear utopian. However, if we do not have a sublime end to life, it is difficult to achieve a necessary mental mutation. Machiavelli, in his book *The Prince,* recommends that archers who are afraid their arrows will not reach the mark aim further than this point. Moderating our personal desires, we intensify our social responsibilities: one cannot have only an individual healing; the illness of others is our illness. Eliminating fleeting things, we fight against the waste that infects consumer society. Together with the deep motto inscribed on the Temple of Apollo, "Know thyself," is another, no less important, "Nothing too much." To discard useless objects, parasitic relationships, and predatory activities is essential to the survival of humanity. Undoing ourselves from mental moorings, eliminating crazy ideas (transmitted by out-of-date religions), having feelings that are foreign to us (copied since childhood from the conflicted emotions of our parents), having desires implanted by industry (sexual dissatisfaction is the basis of unrestrained consumption), and having needs that have no aim other than to make the individual appear to be more than what he or she is (motivated by social neurosis). Instead of obeying the inertia of the past, which deals in "nothing ever changes," we try to deliver the future, which causes both the constant expansion of the universe and the expansion of our own consciousness.

A person who has accomplished the inner work (healing emotional wounds, extolling tolerance, developing listening to others, not getting bamboozled by commercial propaganda or the media, planting positive ideas) and who has learned to be what he truly is and not what others want him to be (loving without discriminating, creating while developing receptivity, existing without self-destruction, feeling grateful for the lifetime granted by the cosmos) can stagnate in an atmosphere of happiness, which is a mistake. In a world where everything advances and expands, to remain immobile is to regress. Consciousness is unlimited; its development is incessant and endless. It is, therefore, recommended that a healthy person fulfill some psychomagic acts once in a while.

USELESS OBJECTS

The objects with which we surround ourselves influence our lives in positive or negative ways. The unconscious gives symbolic significance to things. In our mind these things take on a life-form and act like keys that open old trauma, making them spill out repressed pain or release healing forces. Followers of black magic have used this in a superstitious way to make sinister spells or talismans. Every belonging lying around our homes is accompanied by a memory and occupies a place in our minds, absorbing or giving energy. Useless objects without deep significance—gifts we kept out of obligation, remnants of the past, adornments to fill empty spaces, outdated documents, books we won't read again—absorb our vital energy and our capacity to concentrate, binding us to periods of our lives that we have surpassed. We can call this "spiritual garbage." So that the development of your consciousness occurs without these obstacles, I recommend:

- The consultant gets some adhesive labels and divides them into two groups: one is Yes! The other is No! At midnight on a Sunday, the consultant examines his/her living space and everything in it (furniture, paintings, books, CDs, DVDs, papers, clothes, crockery, trinkets, collections, photographs, diplomas, sheets, and so on). As night passes and dawn comes, the consultant dedicates herself to sticking the labels on everything she sees: Yes! (something useful), No! (something useless). She may have a useful object that comes from a time in which she lived with another partner or which was inherited, without conscious thought, from a dead parent or is a gift tied to the incestuous knot. In these cases, she must also put No! on the object.

At the end of this work, having made the necessary formalities with the corresponding authorities to have this stuff removed, she piles up everything with the No! label and puts it on the street. It makes no difference the value of these useless things; she should not attempt to sell them. If she sells them, the money received and the new objects bought will continue attaching her to this toxic past.

Regarding the remaining useful or essential objects, the Yes! labels, the consultant should say, "Thank you!" She gathers together these labels afterward and makes a ball, puts it in the bottom of a pot, and covers it with dirt and a beautiful flowering plant.

TROUBLESOME MEETINGS

There is a Chinese proverb that says, "In any discussion, the loser is the first to anger." A Hindu legend tells how Buddha's inner peace was so great that the arrows and stones thrown at him by his enemies fell over his body and turned into flowers. The world is what it is, more than what we believe it is: our attitude transforms it. If the consultant must attend a meeting at which he will face adverse opinions that may unleash his anger, I recommend:

- For a few minutes before the meeting, the consultant puts some honey on his ears and gums and rubs it in. This will mix the aggressive words heard with some sweetness, and the harsh words that the consultant wishes to say will soften. Additionally, in order to remember at every moment to proceed in the discussion with measured steps, the consultant should, beforehand, perfume with lavender essential oil the soles of his shoes.

BURN "DEFINITIONS"

"To reach the truth, it is necessary to discard the beliefs they have issued to us and rebuild, from the ground up, all of the systems of our knowledge," wrote Descartes. Although we live, to some degree, peaceful in this world of turmoil, if we want to develop the most of our spirit, we must free ourselves from ideas, beliefs, superstitions, and judgments that the family and society have taught us since childhood. We do not claim that all of these ideas are harmful: some of them can be true. However, as just as these ideas may be, they should not impose onto our consciousness any threatening dogmas. The ideas that they have forced onto us cause behaviors, feelings, and desires that, not being genuinely ours, limit the development of our consciousness.

► The consultant should sit naked at a desk and write on a piece of paper all the ideas that she has of the world and of herself. She mixes together definitions, religious perceptions, orders, political opinions, commonplace truths: "I must do . . . ," "I must not do . . . ," "I think therefore I exist," "If I am not good, I will go to hell," "I have no musical talent," "My mother is never wrong," "Men are immoral," "Ghosts exist," "A virgin woman gave birth to a child-God," and so forth.

Once the consultant has exhausted the number of ideas and beliefs, she will burn these handwritten pages, then dissolve the ashes in condensed milk (an element of infancy and sticky). She must smear this paste on her head and face. The consultant remains seated this way with a fan blowing on her for a half hour. Then the consultant takes a shower, soaping and rinsing the head seven times in a row. The consultant will then go out for an hour wearing a new cap or hat, even though she is not used to wearing such garments. The consultant will then give this hat to a child.

VAMPIRE RELATIONSHIPS

Many individuals have not found a goal toward which to direct their lives; they need to fill up their time. Thinking they are our best friends, they furnish the emptiness of their daily lives with us. They waste a lot of our time with their gossiping, comments on the news, praising themselves, complaining, inviting us to lunch or for drinks, but they are never able to be interested in who *we* are or what *we* deeply feel. They use us like mirrors of their own superficiality. Friendship is to create something positive together: not to kill the other's time. For the consultant who feels socially trapped in this kind of relationship, I recommend:

- On a photograph of one of these "friends," the consultant tapes a strip of black plastic to his or her mouth then puts this photograph face down in the refrigerator. The consultant's unconscious will understand the message, and little by little the consultant will see that, without a big effort, this relationship will go cold.

VAGINAL POWER

When Goddess the Mother was ousted from human culture and the reign of God the Father began, it changed the meaning of basic symbols. The female sun was turned into the male sun and the male moon was turned into the female moon. Before, the sky was female and Earth was male. Today, at the base of our unconsciousness, each time we think of the sky or air, we see the father. And, each time we think of Earth or water, we see the mother.

Some sensitive women who feel oppressed in our world, essentially favoring male values, sometimes have problems breathing: they struggle to breathe in air. Unconsciously, it seems dangerous to let air in the lungs because it, as a symbol of the father, the male, can, from inside the woman's body, invade and enslave them. How are they to fight against a power established since they had use of reason? In order to breathe better, with happiness and trust, I advise the women who suffer from this symptom to carry out the following meditation:

- The consultant lies on her back and bends her knees, placing her heels very close to her buttocks. She opens the knees as wide as possible and tries to breathe deeply, concentrating at the same time on the nose and the vagina. Using her imagination, the consultant should imagine herself inhaling and exhaling at the same time through both her nose and her vagina.

  Little by little, she should let the sensation drop from the nose to the vagina as she imagines that she is breathing exclusively through her vagina.

This exercise will give the woman confidence in herself. She will feel proprietress of air, and she will be able to face men without any fear of being invaded or humiliated.

POETRY

We mustn't confuse things with the words used to name them. The North American psychologist and linguist of Polish origin, Alfred Korzybsky (1879–1950), creator of general semantics and non-Aristotelian logic, said, "The word *dog* does not bite," and "The map is not the land." Words, not being reality but rather a mirror tied to them, should not be confused with truth, which is ineffable and, for its infinite complexity, inconceivable. Names, definitions, and maps are only approximate guides. This disability—caused by articulate speech—has a way of being an exact reproduction of life in a conscious or unconscious way: affecting us and sowing doubts and anxieties. Everyone to some extent realizes that the truth is relative and that what is real is hidden under countless labels. In some way, we are all bitten by the word *dog,* and we all live on maps, never on true lands. The television and other media, in the hands of economic and political interests, doctor their presentation of events. It is one thing to look for the impossible truth, another thing to seek authenticity. The only way to find authenticity is to awaken the essential beauty in ourselves. The medieval alchemists called beauty "the splendor of truth." The majority of illnesses that inflict us come from a lack of consciousness. There is no difference between consciousness and beauty.

To survive in a world that voluntarily keeps its citizens in a state of infancy, it is necessary to introduce beauty into our language, which will affect our feelings, desires, and daily actions. The best method for this is the practice of poetry. This has nothing to do with publishing books or aspiring for applause or prizes, but it has everything to do with writing in secret.

▶ The consultant, for one year, writes a short poem every night. To accomplish this, you must get in the habit of lighting incense (always with the same aroma), listening to inspiring music (always the same music), using the same notebook and the same pencil, and perfuming the soles of the feet and the palms of the hands with the same essence. Nude and alone (without animal or human), the consultant encloses himself in a room, turns off the light, illuminates the page with a beeswax candle, and, imagining that the very last moment of his life has arrived, the consultant writes the most sublime feelings.

In China, long before Buddhism, the citizens were accustomed to writing a poem before the moment of death. In the fifth century, someone sentenced to death wrote:

> when the naked blade nears my head
> it will be like decapitating a spring breeze

A monk who died in the year 568, before dying, wrote:

Lightning's light lasts not long.

Learning each night to die gently revives us the following day to bring beauty into our lives.

TO COMFORT

When we achieve a spiritual equilibrium and have overcome our suffering, we fall into the suffering of others. More than ever, we see the pain of others, the fleetingness of life. We lucidly know that everything we begin ends. This makes us want to comfort all of humanity, which, given its magnitude, is an impossible ideal. However, it is possible to carry out small, comforting gestures. There is a Zen proverb that says: "When a flower opens, it is spring all over the world."

By using minimal amounts of medicine dissolved in a lot of water, healing is accomplished in homeopathy. I recommend:

- The altruistic consultant, each time she sees a person (known or unknown) burdened by problems or, conversely, bragging about something, gives the person a small card, upon which the following sentence is printed:

  This too shall pass.

IMAGINARY OCCUPATION

According to Freud, happiness consists of fulfilling childhood dreams. Children often say, "When I grow up, I will be this or that. I will do this or that." These plans remain registered in the unconscious and harass us all of our lives, transformed into desires to do something extraordinary and impossible. Immersed in the mass of citizens, we yearn to be different, to be someone other than the adult we have become. I recommend:

- The consultant prints business cards with his name on it and a made-up job title that translates to a childhood ideal. The Chilean poet Vicente Huidobro (1893–1948) called himself: "Anti-Poet and Magician." Following this advice, a psychotherapist described himself as "Shadow Cleaner." Other consultants, as their official, imaginary job titles, have claimed to be "Professor of Invisibility," "Rock Hypnotist," "Moral Lifter," "Dreams Diver," "Bonsai Liberator," "Falling Upward Apprentice."

DISIDENTIFICATION

The mysterious occultist Count Alessandro di Cagliostro (1743–1795) was very successful in the court of Louis XVI. He boasted about, among many other things, an ability to make gold, thicken pearls, and increase the size of diamonds. He also boasted about knowing of an elixir used to lengthen a lifetime and resuscitate the dead. He declared that he had spent more than 3,400 years on this planet. To defend himself against accusations that he was a liar, a charlatan, and a hypnotist, he wrote these words, which reveal his high level of consciousness:

> I am not from any era. I am not from anywhere. Outside of time and space, my spiritual being lives an eternal existence. If I sink into my thoughts, tracing the course of ages, if my spirit tends toward a mode of existence away from that which you perceive, I will become what I desire. Don't worry about my nationality, my rank, or my religion.

Something similar is said in the Bible with regard to the high priest, the king of Salem, Melchizedek. A motherless, fatherless king of peace, a king with no genealogy, is described in Hebrews 7:2–3: "King of Salem, which is, king of peace; without father, without mother, without descent, having neither beginning of days nor end of life; but made unto the Son of God."

In some way, Cagliostro and Melchizedek show the road to disidentification from the personal "I." The brain, probably the most complex object in the universe, contains thousands of millions of neurons equipped with a core that functions as a miniature receiver-transmitter apparatus. These cells unite with others, creating circuits that transmit information. A network is gradually woven in contact with our relatives and acquaintances and gives us knowledge. We inherit experiences. However, these experiences, being limited, produce a mental world that covers very few connections: a prison from which we can hardly escape. A baby is born with the ability to speak every language in existence. In the cradle, they make the child into a monolingual being, imprisoning the child in a web of less than one hundred neurons. However, the mysterious energy that circulates through the hundreds of thousands of millions of other neurons intends to create, in our brains, a structure formed by the totality of its cells, the magnificent mind of future man; this is how it tries to connect all consciousness inhabiting the planet. This consciousness, through successive mutations, makes us its instrument of action confronting the familial-social-cultural will, which, in the majority of cases, through the accumulation of inherited ideas, feeling, desires, and needs, opposes the spiritual project and submerges us into low levels of consciousness.

The French theosophist Louis Claude de Saint-Martin (1743–1803) wrote,

> It came to pass, Mighty God, when you ordered light to shine on human beings, the rule of life was in inertia. Light fell upon them but they did not feel it, they were like children sleeping in broad daylight.

In the mother's belly, the fetus already receives orders to imitate the model bequeathed by its ancestors. The family does not accept pure and simple creation as something coming from "nothing" with no exterior model. Instead they limit their children, forcing them to submerge themselves in plans, in slogans ("You will be this or that," "You remind me of such and so," "Obey and propagate our ideas and beliefs"). The main obstacle that we must master in order to go to a higher level of consciousness is the personal "I," an illusion created by the family, society, culture. The authentic essential self fights with this "I" like the angel fought with Jacob (Genesis 32:24–28). From this fight, if left "to dislocate" or lose some of its boundaries, the personal "I" emerges transfigured, free of plans, destiny, projections, or repetitions. Expelling parasitic ideas from the mind, the genius is illuminated; eliminating discrimination, the saint finds emotional peace; mastering the fear of dying, the hero is fulfilled; indulging in strict discipline, the champion wins. When one no longer imitates one's parents and ancestors, recognizing divine consciousness in the mind, emotions and desires, organs and viscera, and living as Cagliostro lived, in eternity and infinity, nothing is mechanical, nothing automatic. Unchanging ideas do not drive this human who is able to stop the internal dialogue, to see each success with the candor and surprise of a child, to open her heart to let sublime feelings bloom, to blow away the ashes of all traditions with quickening breath. The body, impregnated with the soul, after a luminous life, returns the energy it was lent back to the cosmos; the impersonal essence survives individual death.

A "normal" person (someone who lives in accordance with the limitations of the era, as happens with most people) will have enormous difficulties in freeing himself from that which he believes is his individuality. It is possible that some kind of failure, a serious illness, political disillusionment, financial ruin, or the loss of a loved one will submerge the individual in intense suffering in which the personal "I" seems like a mirror broken into a thousand pieces, and so everything loses its meaning; what was thought vanishes. He faces, very reluctantly, the dilemma of death or of rebuilding himself. Various sects re-create this critical state for their followers: some Masonic lodges require the suitor be enclosed in a coffin that contains a sprig of acacia (symbol of eternity), symbolizing death: death to what has been. After some time, when he has come out of the coffin, the individual will be reborn, turned into a new being.

The personal "I" with which we identify has beliefs, intentions, desires, and so forth that imitate those of the family and society but that are not truly authentic: we continuously see the world through the eyes of others. Cagliostro, appearing under this pseudonym, did not identify with a name or a last name nor with an age nor with a sexual definition (he doesn't declare he is a "man" but rather a "being") nor with a religious or political belief nor with a fixed career. It was impossible to define him. The people of that era called him magician. The truth is, from one day to the next, we cannot achieve this state of freedom, but we can start becoming aware of our boundaries. To do this, it is necessary to see from a different point of view, different from "normal."

Above all, if one wishes to bring about a change in the brain, one must develop one's attention span: in reality, we don't completely see, hear, or feel what we perceive internally or externally. The personal "I" acts like deforming glasses: the world it lets us see is, to a large degree, the world they taught us was the world. Below, to evolve our attention spans so that we gradually (but surely) cut ties with the impoverished definitions we have of ourselves, I recommend various psychomagic exercises and acts:

- The consultant draws, on a wall in the house, a black circle the size of a quarter. (It is necessary that this be on a wall and not on a chalkboard or something similar. Symbolically, the house—not a piece of furniture—is the mirror of the whole of the personal "I.") In the middle of this circle, there will be a nearly indiscernible white dot. Every day, as early as possible, the consultant will sit immobile in front of this circle for fifteen minutes, looking at it fixedly and trying to resist allowing any word into the mind. Little by little, if the consultant diligently concentrates, he will see the white dot more and more clearly. When silence is made in the consultant's mind, and the white dot looks big, the consultant will have taken a big step toward becoming his essential being. Each morning, after this short meditation, the consultant goes out for a walk around the block three times, concentrating on an ambulatory prayer, mentally repeating sentences divided into three parts, and each part corresponding to one of the consultant's steps: "I—am—of—you. I—trust—in—you. You—are—my—wellness."

After fulfilling this exercise for a reasonable time frame, the consultant (in order to initiate disidentification), one Friday upon waking up, puts on a mask made with a photograph of his own face and hangs a poster from the neck through which the consultant renounces his name: "I am not Johnny LeValley." Dressed this way, the consultant goes to as many places he frequents as possible—bar, coffee shop, restaurant, bookstore, commercial center, cinema, house of relatives or friends, and so forth—to walk and to observe himself. At 6 p.m., the consultant shuts himself in the house, puts the mask and the poster in a set place, undresses, closes the windows and curtains, disconnects the telephone, turns off the television and computer, and stays there, doing nothing and not listening to music or TV or the radio, completely incommunicable to the outside world. The consultant must not clean or repair anything or rearrange the furniture. It is also prohibited to speak aloud to himself; the consultant must maintain a strict silence. He will eat very little and only raw food: nothing heated up, cooked, or sugary. The consultant will not drink coffee, tea, colas, or liquor or do drugs. This way, without any activity, the consultant will be obligated to see himself.

The consultant lies down to go to sleep at noon, and with the help of an alarm clock, he gets up at 4 a.m. to have breakfast: an infusion and a fruit. This deep experience (facing alone one's limited, personal "I") should end on Monday at 6 p.m.

The morning after, dressed in new clothes, the consultant goes out to the places he visited while carrying the poster and wearing the mask, walking and observing himself until 7 p.m., when he returns home and burns the poster and the mask. The consultant gathers the ashes in an envelope, which he carries in the left inside pocket of his jacket each time he has an important meeting.

To continue defeating his identification with the personal "I," the consultant decides (preferably once per week: for a man, on Tuesday; a woman, Friday) not to pronounce the word *I*. He will carry a fountain pen with red ink in a pocket, and every time the consultant says "I," he will trace a red line on his face.

If the consultant is a very well-known, important person, in order to overcome the danger of taking everything too seriously, once every three months, the consultant should dress like a clown, sit in a public place, and, with a plastic frog or toad, flatter all the small children who get close, telling the boys, "This frog is an enchanted princess," or the girls, "This frog is an enchanted prince."

BECOMING AN ADULT

It is written in the Bible in Genesis 2:24: "Therefore a man shall leave his father and mother and be joined to his wife, and they shall become one flesh." In the Gospel of Matthew 10:37: "He that loveth father or mother more than me is not worthy of me: and he that loveth son or daughter more than me is not worthy of me."

The psychological significance of these sentences makes reference to the need to take the plunge that will carry us from childhood to adulthood. The esoteric philosopher G. I. Gurdjieff affirmed that human beings are not born with a whole soul but rather with a seed of the soul for which they must care and which must grow throughout their lives. This requires hard, spiritual work. He said, "Whomever does not carry out this work lives like a pig and dies like a dog."

Birth, with a sublime but foreign element embedded in our bodies, like an olive in a martini, is difficult for us to accept. It seems less spooky to think that we were born with a small consciousness we must develop—increasingly demolishing its boundaries, until it and reality have an identical expanse. Leaving out the pigs and dogs, it is better to say: "Whoever doesn't do this work will live childishly and will die unfulfilled."

This is precisely the purpose of psychomagic: remove the consultant from the psychological prison into which the family has shoved her so that, in this way, she will not repeat the ills that limit her predecessors. This is extremely difficult work because the defects that have been bequeathed to us constitute our "individuality," our personal ego, which we confuse with our essential being. This individuality is basically made out of an infantile point of view toward ourselves and toward the exterior world, an infantilism that persists into old age by the rigid custom of calling our parents, not by their first names, but by the words *mama* and *dada*. The majority of mothers plant these sounds in their children when they give them an order or advice. They never say, "I command you" or "I advise you" but "Mama says" or "Dada says." It is normal for young ones, until the onset of puberty, to have need for powerful archetypes for which it is absolutely necessary to call their parents "Mama" and "Dada." If this didn't occur, they would feel incomplete, without protection. But, at the age of thirteen (the age at which primitive tribes subject the children to rites of passage through which they shed their progenitors in order to then turn into adults), this way of being led by the parents should be abandoned. If it doesn't stop, the individual will never feel like an adult. Psychomagic proposes the following ceremony for the consultant:

- On the child's thirteenth birthday, she will be celebrated at a family reunion at which the mother will offer a rectangle of marzipan on which the word *mama* is written in sugar and the father will offer the same thing with the word *dada* written on it in sugar. The child should eat it, then the parents will tell her, "You have entered into our world of adults. From now on, without losing respect, you should try to treat us not like gigantic symbols but like beings similar to you. You should call us by our names." Then the mother will give the child a nice gift and ask the child to thank her, using the new method, saying: "Thank you, [the mother's first name]." The father gives the child another gift and makes the same request, and the child agrees, saying: "Thank you, [the father's first name]." The parents will reply, "From now on, if you call us 'Mama' or 'Dada,' we won't answer you. If you call us by our first names, we will be entirely at your disposal."

If it is an adult who wants to free himself from these two, infantilizing words, deeply embedded in the mind:

- The consultant will write "mama" and "dada" on a rock that weighs at least three pounds and go down a dirt road (if possible) a little way out of town. He will move forward by throwing the rock as far in front of him as possible, then picking it up and taking three steps and throwing it again as far as possible. This should be continued for three miles. Then he buries the rock after covering it with honey.

FOUR

Psychomagic Consultations

What Lies Hidden in the Darkness of the Unconscious?

The psychomagic advice in the first part of this book can be applied to any problem suffered as indicated in the consultation title; however, it is necessary to adapt the actions, with some changes, to the character of each individual and to the configurations of each person's genealogy tree. Whoever wishes to delve into these techniques with the purpose of prescribing acts to others or to him- or herself, I present here some of the numerous consultations I did in 2007 and in the café in Paris where I read the Tarot every Wednesday. During my five-hour consulting sessions, each meeting with each of the thirty-plus people I saw lasted no more than eight minutes. The Tarot, used as a psychological test, combined with a definite intuitive evolution acquired thanks to more than thirty years of study, allows me to go without force directly to the consultant's essential problem, gently finding a door in the consultant's defensive wall. Generally, whoever suffers does not wish to know *why* he or she suffers but only wants to *get rid* of his or her painful symptoms. Illnesses and psychological suffering are essentially caused by a lack of consciousness. The cause of injury is so painful that it is hidden in the darkness of the unconscious. In combat, warriors strenuously fight to kill the enemy. In a Tarot session, one fights strenuously to return the other to life. At the beginning of my readings, sometimes this combat is made by using a lot of violence.

I tell of this attitude, which I learned from my Zen meditation teacher, Ejo Takata (1928–1997), in my book *El Maestro y Las Magas.* When I learned that it is one thing to give and another to force someone to receive, I then began to move forward on a sweet and compassionate path. I eliminated from my heart all types of discrimination; I expelled from my soul the unforgiving judge who wielded a morality based on poorly translated and poorly interpreted religious texts. For the duration of these consultations, I forgot myself and concentrated totally on the person in front of me. I opened my mind, motivated only by the desire to be useful and to offer a loving ear, to accept any rejection with kindness, seeing it as an important part of the healing process.

Psychomagic is not a scientific discipline; it is an artistic creation of theatrical origin, which tends to awaken the creativity in the consultant, turning the consultant into his or her own healer. This longtime activity was useful for me, too. Naturally, little by little, I was opening the gate that was between my intellect and my unconscious. Barely revealing the source of the problem, without the least effort, I reach the psychomagic act, with the client's corresponding astonishment, because, upon my stating the act, something seemingly impossible, surreal, or absurd corresponded with what the consultant was experiencing. I told an elegant, stylish gentleman, "Get close to your young son. You should invite him on a motorcycle ride." And this gentleman told me he had just bought a motorcycle. I advised a woman to ride on a horse then rub the beast's sweat on her, and she told me she owned a riding school. In both of these consultations, the consultants smiled with relief upon hearing the act I advised. This was precisely what they came looking for. If you, the reader, can identify with the consultant's problem, and the act I propose resonates with you, you can do it, adapting it to your own reality. If, for example, I speak of visiting a grave, the loved one could be in a burial place or may have been cremated: it doesn't change the act, whether it is carried out at a grave site or where the ashes were scattered. Sometimes something very difficult is asked. How does one ask an adult to find a woman who is nursing who will let him nurse? Although the consultant often rejects this act, one must insist. If a person is persistent and has faith, everything he seeks comes to him. Modifying the proverb "If the mountain doesn't come to you, then go to the mountain," we must say, with fervor, "I am not going to the mountain, but I wish with all of my soul that the mountain will come to me."

The psychologist Jacques Lacan (1901–1981), during a class, told his students, "In a moment of creative ecstasy, first talk and then think." The messages from the unconscious have the spontaneity of dreams. They are not created by the intellect. The person prescribing a psychomagic act first receives it from the unconscious then recommends it, just as it is dictated by the unconscious. Explications, products of the rational mind, clarify some aspects of the act but do not exhaust its mystery.

I ask each consultant, if he or she carries out the suggested act, to then send me a card telling me the details of the experience and the result obtained. So the reader can see how these encounters develop, I've included a response below, which describes a consultation I had with a pregnant woman who wanted to have a normal and happy delivery but whose physician threatened her with a cesarean section:

> We went to see you on the 10th of October, 2007, my wife and I, accompanied by our four-year-old son. Noticing my wife was pregnant, you asked her:

"This is your second? What is the first one named?"

"Ethan."

"And the second, what name will you give him?"

"Nathan."

"That is a mistake! It is too similar to Ethan. If you want your son to have his own individuality, choose another name. Why are you here for Tarot?"

"I am going to deliver in the next two weeks. My son is upside down. My doctor says he will be forced to remove him by way of cesarean. My husband, who is a psychotherapist, and I know very well why this occurs. I am afraid of repeating the same atrocious pain of my first delivery, which we wanted to be a girl, not a boy. I feel like my husband is starting to act like my father and also my psychologist. This is a great awareness but it doesn't serve me, practically, to avoid the cesarean. Do you think, with a psychomagic act, we can get the child to turn to the correct position?"

You recommended the following:

- Ethan plays the role of his future brother. You, being the doctor, place him over the mother's naked body, in the fetal position with the head up. Guiding the child with chocolates, turn the child over the stomach, slowly, delicately, until his head is turned down. Then you, Mrs., mimic the birth, having him slide softly between your legs. Before carrying out this act, find another name for your son.

I waited for my wife to find another name from deep within her. For three days, she looked for names very similar, phonetically, to Ethan. On the fourth day, she found it: Luke!

Finally, we were able to fulfill the act: Ethan seemed happy to play the role of his little brother. Mother and son were nude. I put my son on his mother's stomach and began to give him chocolates while he delicately, slowly, with precaution, started turning himself around. He laughed and ate chocolates. After fifteen minutes, he was in the correct position and my wife mimicked an easy, agreeable, happy delivery. We said hello to our son, "Welcome to the world, Luke!" While hugging and kissing, our son ate his last and ninth chocolate.

The miracle! Little by little, the fetus turned, and when the big moment arrived, my wife gave birth in total serenity, without an epidural and without the slightest problem. Our doctor and the midwife were so amazed that they refused to charge us for their services.

107 PSYCHOMAGIC ACTIONS AND OUTCOMES

In all of the examples presented here, the consultants who fulfilled the psychomagic acts obtained the hoped-for result.

1. A woman has bad relations with men. Her conflict originates in the negative image that her mother gave her.

▶ I recommended that she dress completely in her mother's clothes and then talk to her lover as if she were her mother, repeating all the negative concepts she received in her childhood. I told her to let the words of hate, which her mother inoculated in her, arise in her mouth. After she insults her partner, she tears these clothes to pieces while screaming, "I am not her! I am capable of loving you!" She then sends the rags, smeared in honey, in a gift box to her mother.

2. A young woman gets extremely nervous when she drives a car and, because of this, she is forced to drive only rarely.

▶ I recommended driving, dressed as a little girl, accompanied by her parents. Her mother should have a packet of candies and put one in her mouth every five minutes while her father, also every five minutes, should whisper in her ear, "Women drive better than men."

3. A childless woman, who forgot the first eight years of her childhood, is afraid she has developed uterine cancer. She was born after her mother aborted the previous pregnancy at three months. The consultant's father abandoned the home when the consultant's mother was three months pregnant with her. She explains that her birth was not desired. Lacking individuality, she identified with her mother, and she feels possessed by the sacrificed fetus, which she feels has materialized into cancer.

▶ I recommended that she fill a red bag with candies and go distribute them to the children in an orphanage. She then carries the bag for seven days with a kitchen knife painted black in it, and then hides it, after seven days, somewhere in her mother's house without telling her.

The red bag represents her desires to live; the black knife, the mother's wishes to abort her as she did with her brother. The guilt over having disobeyed by being born makes her create cancer, a tumor that represents when she was in the fetal state. All of this is returned to the parent.

4. A woman asks why she creates obstacles all the time. Through the Tarot, I explain to her that she reproduces the obstacles that her father put in her way. These difficulties, in the absence of affection (he wanted a boy not a girl), were the only thing that united her to him. The consultant confirmed the reading, revealing that she still keeps the father's ashes in an urn.

▶ I recommended that she dress as a man and go to a rugby game (a sport her father loved and to which he never wanted to take her), carrying the urn. She should watch the whole game and, at the end, empty the father's ashes in the seat in which she was sitting. Then she should bury the man's suit and plant an orchid over it.

5. A blind man cannot stand that his mother treats him like a handicapped child. He wants me to give him a psychomagic act to help him express his huge rage.

▶ I recommended that he stand in front of his mother with a bull's eye in each hand, screaming, "Look!" then he should throw the eyes at her and scream, "Eat them!" Then, putting a rock album on at high volume, he should undress and say, between laughter, "Now do you see! I am a man!"

6. A young woman can't manage to have an orgasm with her lover. In general, she is afraid of men. Her father was assassinated by the mafia in Palermo.

▶ I recommended that she enroll in a shooting club, then buy a pistol with which her lover masturbates her until she reaches orgasm. Then she buries the pistol with a photo of her father and a wedding ring.

7. An old man, crying, solicits an act that will get him out of the depression from which he has suffered for more than twenty years. He feels that his ex-wife, his daughter (now older), and his mother abuse him because, although they constantly ask him for money, they also won't quit blaming him for ruining his marriage.

▶ I recommended that he invite his ex-wife, his daughter, and his mother to dinner at his home. At the table, there will be three plates of black metal, without covers. He will put on each plate a whole, roasted chicken. He will take out a hammer and destroy the three chickens, screaming with frightening fury, "Stop it! Stop it! Stop it!" Then he will present three containers filled with earth, ordering them to bury the pieces of chicken. Then he will give each one a flowering plant to plant in a pot. He will then tell them, "Get out of here! From now on, when you want to have dinner with me, you will have to pay the tab."

8. A woman asks how she can make her father quit depending on her. He makes her responsible for all the dealings in the outside world while he waits for her at home, cleaning and cooking. I explain that she is living not as a daughter but as a wife to her father, a couple in which she has the role of the man and he has the role of the woman.

► I recommended that she tell her father that she is going to give him a pair of handmade shoes and that, for these, he must take action: he has to stand on a sheaf of paper and draw the contour of his feet with a pencil. She gives these drawings to a master shoemaker so that he can concoct a pair of women's shoes with tall heels. Once finished, she brings the shoes to her father saying, "I will continue to worry over you only if you use these shoes here in the house and also when you go out shopping or visiting your friends. If I am your man, you should assume the role of my wife."

9. The consultant has a problem with his father: he despises him for being dirty. He is ashamed to tell his girlfriend that his father is a garbage man.

► I recommended that he go to the girlfriend dressed in his father's dirty clothes with his face stained with soot. He isn't to speak as himself but as if he were his own father: "I have come to tell you something in the name of my son because he dared not confess it because he is ashamed of me. He didn't want you to know that I am a dirty garbage man. With pleasure I will quit this job, but I need it to pay for his education. He loves you deeply. I should tell you he is a good boy, studious, intelligent, and at the base, he loves me as much as I love him. To end this problem, could you do me the favor of washing me?" Then he asks the girlfriend to undress him and wash him. Then, dressed in his own clothes (that he brought in a package), he will go with her to introduce her to his father.

10. The consultant is an osteopath interested in shamanism. His mother had cancer in the right knee. He believes this trouble has a psychological origin. At the death of her husband, she, clad in her widowhood because men have disappointed her, allows only her son to visit her. She doesn't want to see any doctors. She demands that he cure her. He doesn't know how to.

▶ I recommended that he make a placebo surgery. He should buy a squid and then go visit his mother. He should then draw the curtains closed to prevent the light from entering and, with the house totally dark, light some candles and a lot of incense. He places his mother's knee over a pillow, washes the knee with blessed water, compresses the squid forcefully against the cancer for at least ten minutes, and tells her, "This is your cancer; I am going to remove it." The consultant takes a bladeless knife and mimics removing the squid-cancer with great difficulty. With his performance, he should convince his mother, and in this way, she will believe that he struggles mightily to remove her cancer. After an intense struggle, he rips out the squid-cancer. Then, lighting it with candles, he goes to the bathroom, accompanied by his mother, and shows her as he throws the "cancer" into the toilet bowl. She should flush the toilet. He gives her a very nice perfume so that each day she can spray perfume on her knee.

11. A consultant, a native of Barcelona and the daughter of very Catholic parents, suffers from a very solid fear of being assassinated. Through the Tarot, I explain to her that this fear is not of being murdered by some unknown but by herself because of her sexual desires. Her parents raised her for the order, hoping for an intact holy hymen.

► I recommended that she stroll along the boulevards dressed as a nun, serendipitously giving each man a pornographic photograph: it will work just as well to buy one in the sex shop and photocopy it. After distributing one hundred photos, she sends the nun's suit to her parents, accompanied by a box of one hundred condoms.

12. A fifty-year-old woman has a lot of difficulty asking for what she needs emotionally, especially of her partner (to whom she has been married for thirty years). Thanks to the Tarot, she remembers when she was little that she was interned in the hospital with tuberculosis and no relative visited her. She understands that this is the cause of the difficulty she has expressing herself to her partner.

► I recommended that she, for whatever false motive, check herself into a private clinic early one morning. She waits, lying down, for her visitors. She expresses the pain of feeling abandoned. Four hours later, her husband arrives, bringing her flowers, chocolates, and a rag doll. He kisses her and puts a candy in her mouth, undresses her, rubs the doll all over her body, and then makes love to her. They then go from the clinic to a bar to get drunk and celebrate.

13. A woman has problems at work with her very aggressive boss. She says that her father would verbally attack her mother. She realizes that she has always established amorous relationships with aggressive men who pull her down and whom she ends up insulting until they feel insignificant.

▶ I recommended an act that lasts two and a half months, always done anonymously. The first day of the first month, she enters her boss's office when he is not there and leaves a little box of chocolates in his desk. Fifteen days later, she does the same thing but with a larger box of chocolates. The first day of the second month she again leaves an even bigger box of chocolates. Fifteen days later, she leaves another even larger box. Finally, in the middle of the third month, leaving the biggest box yet, she invents a way to surprise her boss. She gives him this explanation: "I realized my behavior toward you was aggressive." From this point on, he will treat her better.

14. The consultant is a military pilot. During a battle, he was shot down and made prisoner. Since his return, he can't stop being in conflict with his bosses because he believes they discount him. He is an instructor, and he doesn't want to change his career or environment. He says see that his father was also a military pilot, but he was never taken prisoner. He realizes that because of this mishap, he feels that he has shamefully betrayed the trust his father placed in him.

▶ I recommended that he should rent a small plane and take his whole family for a ride: his wife, son, and father (who should sit to his right). Fifteen minutes after takeoff, in midflight, his father should hug him, kiss him on the mouth, and pin a medal to his chest. This will persuade his unconscious that his father does accept him, and the consultant's professional situation will get better.

15. A young man who, thanks to his mother, has studied piano since he was a child living in Barcelona works in something that he doesn't like but that makes him a lot of money. He is afraid that if he dedicates himself entirely to music, he will die of hunger. His father would tell him, "If you are an artist, you will not earn enough money, and you will turn into a beggar!"

► I recommend that he should go to La Rambla, the main street in Barcelona, with an electric piano and play for hours with a poster that reads: "I am not a beggar! *Do not give me money!* I play the piano for pleasure!"

16. A woman who has suffered with genital herpes for twenty years wants to know if it has a psychological cause and how to cure it. Reading her Tarot, I tell her that this illness is the consequence of sexual abuse. The consultant says this is what her therapist said after four years of work. The abuse, by her father, happened when she was still a baby.

► I recommended that she, dressed as a baby, suck a lollipop while she makes love very delicately with her husband who wears an undershirt with her father's face printed on it and his sex smeared with rose marmalade. They should repeat this experience for a week in order to calm and to satisfy the little girl inside her.

17. A young man (who never knew his father) is in love with an older man and has lived with this man, as his lover, for six months. The young man's partner, discovering that he had been unfaithful, kicked him out, changed the locks, and promised that he would never unlock the door again. This made the young man sad. "What can I do to make him take me back?" the young man asked. I learned that the ex-lover's birthday is in a month.

► I recommended that he order two birthday cakes: a big one and a miniature one. On both cakes, a "70" (the lover's age) will be written in sugar. Three days before his ex-lover's birthday, the young man will take the smaller cake to his ex-lover's house and leave it at his door with a card on which will be written, "This is a shrunken copy of the big cake that I will bring to you on your birthday. My love for you grows day by day." If done this way, the young man will receive what he desires.

18. The consultants, a man and a woman, have been together for fifteen years. They began their relationship when they were very young. They do not live together, and they have no children. She is an only child and lives with her father, a widower. He is an only child, also, and lives with his mother, a widow. They realize this is the problem.

▶ I recommended that in order to free themselves, they rent, in the greatest secrecy, a small apartment. In this love nest, they will meet often. They should make two medallions: for him, one with a photo of his mother that she will wear when they make love; for her, one with a photo of her father that he will wear when they make love. They keep track of how often they make love. After forty times, they bury the medallions in two separate pots and plant flowers over them. She gives her potted plant to her father, and he gives his to his mother. After this, they will find it easy to live together. They will always organize it so that when the mother visits, so does the father: the couple will refuse to see them separately.

19. A woman wants to find love and form a partnership, but she always finds men who won't commit. She is conscious of the fact that she does everything possible to drive them away. We see that her mother, obsessively religious, has lived alone since giving birth to this woman and has never managed to find a partner.

▶ I recommended that she go to a shop specializing in selling religious artifacts and buy a human-sized statute of a saint—Saint Pio, for example—which she will offer to her mother saying, "I had some irresistible desires to buy you this saint." (With this, the unconscious, accompanied by "a man," will overcome the prohibition and fulfill what the mother was unable to fulfill.)

20. The lower part of the body of the consultant's father (now seventy-six years old) was paralyzed one month before the consultant's birth. His mother (now sixty-nine years old) took care of him. A brother died of cancer when he was thirteen years old, one year before the consultant's birth. The father, feeling guilty for the death of his son (perhaps because he wished for it), no longer wanted to live and castrated himself by way of his paralysis. The mother used the consultant for comfort and replaced the dead one with him, and the consultant feels sapped by his deceased sibling as well as fearful of being struck by cancer.

▶ I recommended that he should learn how to make objects out of plastic or plaster. With his own hands, he should make a skeleton of a thirteen-year-old child. His brother played the electric guitar and wanted to play music and give concerts. Carrying the skeleton on his back, he attends a rock concert. Getting close to the stage, the consultant puts the skeleton at the feet of the musicians and, in this way, presents these fake bones as an offering to the musicians. Afterward, he visits his father, and turning the volume up to blast rock music, the consultant dances around naked in front of him. In the middle of this frenzy, he takes his father in his arms and says, "Dance with me, not with my brother!" After this, he accepts his obvious homosexuality and finds a lover, who he will introduce to his mother and father.

21. A young man with long hair sits in front of me and says nothing. I notice that he has very long nails on the left hand and very short nails on the right hand. The Tarot reading speaks of his duality. He feels on his right hand his masculinity and on his left hand his femininity.

I think that his mother, through him, wanted to make him a perfect man who wanted what she was; whereas, as an introjection of his mother, he wanted to be the perfect woman. He is immersed in the conflict of not being a man or a woman.

► I recommended that he sit on the terrace of a café and ask for peppermint schnapps (feminine green) and a grenadine (masculine red) and, drinking a little sip of one and then the other, observe the men and women passing, concentrating with total freedom only on their sexual energy. He will give himself the freedom to look, which will allow him to accept himself just as he is.

22. A consultant shows me a photograph of his mother so that she will heal from a persistent, infected wound that she has in the left hand. I explain that the left hand may symbolize the maternal grandmother and that if his mother cannot cure the infection it is because, although her mother (his grandmother) is already dead, the consultant's mother still requests help from her mother: help that was given to her during childhood.

► I recommended that his mother go to the cemetery and rub her infected hand, covered in honey, over the grandmother's tomb or gravestone. Once this act is done, the wound will heal.

23. A very virile, rough-looking man, without wanting to specify much, says he has problems in his sexual life. I tell him, according to the cards he chose, that I think his father raped him when he was young. The consultant, bursting into tears, tells me, "It is a secret I've kept for years!" His father was a policeman.

► I recommended that he should dress in a uniform similar to his father's. Immediately after, he should dress in his wife's clothes and have anal sex with her (with her approval beforehand). Then he should burn the uniform and the clothes, gather together the ashes, and spread them at the door of the police station.

24. The consultant is unable to form a partnership, having had a father who verbally abused her, saying, "You are a bitch!" She feels a deep aggression toward men.

▶ I recommended that she go to a veterinarian to get the jaw of a deceased dog. Tearing out the teeth, she should make a collar that she should wear each time she leaves the house. This will allow her to express her rage symbolically and will change her attitude. She will give the collar to a man she likes.

25. A woman appears with a leather jacket that is too big for her. When I ask her who the garment belongs to, she says, "I bought it second hand but it looks like something of my father's." She says that when she was little, she was very bad, undisciplined and disrespectful, and threatened him with a knife. She was put in a correctional facility. She doesn't have a career. She lives with the guilt. She wants to know how she can forgive herself.

▶ I recommended that she take classes to learn to be a clown and then to go entertain children in the hospitals.

26. A light-skinned man of Haitian origin is dissatisfied with his body; he feels discriminated against, and he wants to change his identity. He is a musician.

▶ I recommended that he should walk around in a busy part of the city in which he lives, with his body painted a pale color. Then sit on the terrace of a café and play a melody on his flute. Then he should return home and cover his skin with a very black makeup. He should repeat the above scenario, sitting again at the café and playing his song again. Finally, the third time, he should repeat everything, without paint, in his natural skin color.

27. A married man experiences violent back pains every night.

▶ I recommended that he ask his wife to caress him, rubbing his back with the lips of her sex while singing a lullaby. After three of these "vagina massages" the pain will disappear.

28. A female consultant, who holds back enormous fury, wants to be rid of it. She had a domineering mother who, with rigid severity, forced the consultant, who had minor scoliosis, to wear a back brace from ages five to fifteen. This is the reason why the consultant lives repressing her femininity.

▶ I recommended that the consultant buy a baseball bat, a back brace for children, and a box of chocolates in the shape of hearts. She then goes to see her mother to tell her, "Sit down. I am going to perform for you." She gives her the chocolates to eat during the show in which the consultant violently beats the back brace with the bat, verbalizing all of the suffering guarded in her memory. Then the consultant should throw the back brace out the window, return to her home, paint the baseball bat gold, and hang it on the wall as an ornament.

29. A single, Jewish mother, for no apparent reason, has an enormous anxiety that her only son is going to die at the end of his thirteenth year. Through the Tarot, I tell her that she actually is not afraid of her son dying but that he will become an adult: that is to say, he will begin to have his own life, and he will sooner or later leave her and go away with his wife. The consultant adds that, after his birth, she wasn't able to earn money like she was when she was a single woman.

▶ I recommended that she organize a ritual to celebrate her son's passage from child to adult. She should make sure ten men attend and that they each approach the young man with a $50 bill in their hands. One by one, they give him the bills, after each one shakes him as if to expel something from his body. And they continue like that until the boy has all ten bills. Then they congratulate him for being a man now. Now, alone with her son, she tells him, "They have given you $500. I want to make you a business proposition. I will add another $500. That way, you will have a thousand dollars to make a profitable business playing the stock market."

30. A woman lives alone with her six-year-old son. She is separated from the son's father, a successful businessman. After many lawsuits, he bought them a little apartment of about four hundred square feet. Taking advantage of this purchase, he stopped paying alimony. The consultant wants to know what she should do in order to obtain what is fair.

▶ I recommended that she write a card to her ex-husband saying, "Your son is six years old, and he loves you very much. You know that we have to feed him well. I think you have a lot of problems with money because you ceased his child support. As I know you are a good human being, I am going to help you by sending you $50 per month. Forgive me, but it is what I can do at the moment in my stretched economic situation. You have been so generous with your son, and I want to help you until you solve your problems."

31. A woman who knows the mediocre life she is living is no longer working realizes that she needs to leave everything and begin a new stage. But, due to inertia, fear, or an absurd feeling of responsibility, she can't manage to break ties, and she asks me how to do this.

▶ I recommended that she go to the main street in the city in a wheelchair and, one hour per day, for seven continuous days, whine bitterly. If people ask her why she is crying like that, she will respond, "Because I died yesterday!"

32. A man comes to consult me because each time he makes love, after ejaculating, he has pain in his penis. No doctor has been able to find a cause for this pain. Through the Tarot I see that in childhood, his mother, a religious fanatic, always told him that he would be a priest when he grew up.

▶ I recommended that he go see his mother dressed as a priest and tell her, "I know now that I should end my sex life and become a priest. This, of course, makes you happy. But this hurts me." Then he undresses and stands nude in front of her and says, "Look at this sex God gave me. Respect it and bless it because I am not a priest but a man who is going to give you grandchildren." The consultant should convince her to accompany him to bury the suit and plant a small fruit tree over it.

33. A man says he was locked in a Turkish bath and risked scalding himself to death. Since this accident, he lives overwhelmed by a strange anxiety. Through the Tarot we see that he was born in the tenth month covered in a skin rash because of his lack of amniotic liquid. As the result of the difficult labor of his birth, his mother was ill for many years. They blamed him for having been too large to exit the cervix. This caused him to have a failure neurosis. The incident in the Turkish bath revived his initial anxiety.

▶ I recommended that he go out on the street on foot-high stilts, dressed as a baby. He tells the people who look at him, "I am a big baby and this makes me happy!" Then he proceeds to distribute candies to children.

34. A man wants to know why, after having studied to be a healer, learning tai chi, do-in, acupuncture, and reiki, he decides not to practice it. We see through the Tarot that his parents didn't pay attention to him (he was an abandoned baby), and he barely notices himself. He lacks faith.

► I recommended that he should travel to Lourdes, France. When he gets six miles away from the grotto, he starts to cry and gathers his tears in a small glass. When he arrives at the grotto, he pours these tears into the sacred fountain and implores the Virgin, "Give me faith in myself!"

35. A man writing a theater piece has problems finishing the second act. He feels blocked. Each time he tries to advance, after writing a few pages, he is driven to tear them up and throw them in the garbage. Together with this creative block, he has problems defecating: he does so with difficulty every three days. Thanks to the Tarot we see that this is a childhood problem: his mother always complained of not being capable of having a second child. She lost every pregnancy. The consultant identifies with the mother, "aborting" his second act. Impeding his creating impedes his defecating.

► I recommended that when he defecates he should clean himself with the white pages of his second act. Then he should write whatever he wants to, beginning on these soiled pages. Then he should put the pages in a leather box that he seals with red sealing wax. He will entrust this box to his mother saying, "I want you to keep this for me for nine months." At the end of this time, the consultant recovers the box and buries it, planting two plants above it: one big one, the other small. If this is done, there will be no problem writing the second act or anything else.

36. A woman doubts the possibilities for success and cannot complete her projects. She has a complex because she looks like her father, but she is not a man. She overvalues the masculine power.

▶ I recommended that she should buy a very feminine handbag and, from a sex shop, acquire a large phallus that she should paint gold. She should walk around town carrying this phallus in her handbag. Each time she goes to urinate, she takes out the phallus and crosses herself with it, reciting, "Our Mother who art in heaven, thy will be done here on Earth." Then she puts the phallus in her handbag and tells it, "Quiet! You obey me!"

37. A lesbian cannot separate from her domineering mother.

▶ I recommended that she should show handcuffs to her mother. Then, as a game, the consultant handcuffs herself to her mother. This way, wrist to wrist, the two shouldn't separate for a whole day. As much as her mother might protest, become furious, exasperated, or cry, the consultant does not unlock the cuffs. At the end of the day, the consultant demands that her mother unlock the cuffs in the company of the whole family, at which time they greet the consultant's beloved. Once in front of the whole family, carrying a large kitchen clock, the consultant and her beloved announce that they will kiss one another for ten minutes and that the family should let them know when the time is up. The lovers complete the task then distribute oval-shaped candies to everyone.

38. A well-built man arrives with a mastiff that he treats very sweetly. He teaches kendo (a kind of Japanese martial art fought with a sword). After many years of practice, he has obtained a seventh *dan* (a dan, or rank, is a scale of titles awarded to the practitioners). His greatest ambition is to obtain the eighth rank, which is the highest rank. For this, he must go to Japan. The official commission that grants these degrees requires enormous quality of its participants, but if the person who solicits this rank is a foreigner, the tests he or she is required to undergo are virtually impassable. He asks me for a psychomagic act in order to pass the tests.

▶ I recommended that he should put his wisdom to practice and that he split his dog in two in his training room. He left without saying a word. At the end of a week, he returned (as is customary), accompanied by his dog. He thanked me, saying, "I realized that, for all these years, I have practiced kendo only for the pleasure of combat and not so they will give me any honorary titles. Having diminished my desires to obtain the eighth dan, I didn't need to murder this poor dog."

39. A young man, accompanied by his lover, feels like a prisoner because his mother, whenever he is absent, emotionally blackmails him with a crying spell. He wants to go live with his beloved, but he can't separate from his mother. His father was run over by a car. Since then, as the only son, he has lived with his widowed mother. She holds him prisoner, fearing that the accident will be replicated.

▶ I recommended that he park his car in front of his house and honk the horn excessively until his mother appears in the window. He sprays himself with three gallons of fake blood and lies under the car, leaving his head and arms out. He screams, "I am not my father! I will not die like him because I love a woman!" He should then get up, get in his car (where his lover waits for him), and, still bloodied, begin to make love to her. Afterward, they get out of the car and go into the house. He introduces his lover to his mother, saying, "This is my girlfriend. Bless us because we are going to get married!"

40. A pianist, with a baby voice and childish movements, wants to compose songs but can't manage to develop his creativity. Because his mother hates men, he (so that she won't hate him) acts like an asexual child. He must understand that creativity is closely aligned with sexual energy.

▶ I recommended that he should burn a photograph of his mother, take a pinch of the ashes, and dissolve it in a glass of milk to drink. Then he should masturbate while hitting the piano keys with his phallus, ejaculating and smearing his sperm on them.

41. A woman whose parents fight all the time doesn't know how to quit being verbally aggressive. Each time a man tries to seduce her, she covers him in insults.

▶ I recommended that she should buy (in a gag shop) plastic teeth and then wear them. She goes to a café and sits on the terrace with a bowl of yogurt and honey. Taking a pair of pliers from her handbag, she theatrically begins a painful fight to remove the false teeth. After three huge efforts and cries, they are extracted. Then she caresses her gums, teeth, tongue, and the roof of her mouth with the honey-yogurt. Following this, she takes a walk and kisses the first man who looks kindly at her.

42. A man who has a beautiful voice and who dreams of dedicating himself to theater cannot do it because he suffers with a debilitating timidity that prevents him from speaking in public.

▶ I recommended that he should make a two-foot-long tube, paint it, varnish it, change it into a beautiful object, and, carrying the tube, go to a museum of modern art dressed like an angel (white tutu, a mane of blonde hair, a pair of wings). He then requests that a museum visitor allow him to whisper something very beautiful in the visitor's ear—clarifying that it is not for money but to cultivate his art. With the visitor's consent, he puts the tube to the visitor's ear and recites a poem into it from the other side. He should repeat this with as many visitors as possible. At the end of the day, the consultant will feel accepted. He will have overcome his timidity.

43. A woman confesses that ten years ago her boyfriend raped her. She didn't defend herself and let him do what he wanted. She never wanted to see him again. After this, she hasn't had an emotional or a sexual life. I asked her the boyfriend's name. "Alberto." "And your father?" "Alfonso." I have her notice how both names begin with the same letter. In her unconscious is the impression of having been raped by her father. This provokes a feeling of guilt because it reveals her incestuous wishes.

▶ I recommended that a friend should wait for her in a public park on a bench, wearing a mask made with a photo of the father's face. She should arrive dressed as a little girl. She should sit on the ground in front of him and tell him, "Daddy, I should confess something: I wanted to be your girlfriend and marry you. I wanted you to throw yourself on top of me and possess me just like you do with Mama. I was a little girl. Forgive me." The friend should say, "I understand you, and I forgive you." Then, disguised that way, they should go to a café and have a refreshing drink and pastries. Then she will bury the mask of her father and the little girl costume and plant a rosebush.

44. A man, though he has lived many years in another country to be far away from his invasive mother, still feels her presence in his mind, preventing him from finding a partner and starting a family.

► I recommended that he buy a plastic cord and wind it around his waist four times. At the end of the cord, he should attach a photograph of his mother. He should wear it like that for four days, during which time he should not bathe. At the end of this time, he sends the cord and the photograph to her by mail along with scissors and a card that reads: "Those who take back lied when giving. Thank you for having given me life."

45. A consultant feels depressed after receiving an insulting and threatening card.

► I recommended he wrap the card in raw meat and toss it onto an anthill.

46. An artist/painter feels like he is not the social character others think he is. He feels like he doesn't have anything to say and that none of his paintings are sincere and that he only paints to sell or to receive applause from snobbish people. He hates his way of life. He wants to turn into a real man.

► I recommended that he should prepare ten masks with ten photographs of his face. Before wearing them—one after the other—he makes his face up as a skull. He goes out masked like this to ten places. Each time he goes to one of these places, he removes the mask, breaks it into little pieces, and tosses it like rain over a child's head. After destroying nine masks, he returns home and destroys the tenth one in front of a mirror, where he will contemplate his skull face for one hour. Then he will remove the makeup, throw his paintings out the window, change his name, and send out a newsletter to everyone he knows, telling them that the painter D (the consultant's name) has died and that the human being E (the consultant's new name) has been born.

47. A man tells of a trauma with his mother: she terrorized him, hitting him on the head with a rolled-up newspaper. In spite of being thirty years old, he is still afraid of her. I asked him what kind of newspaper his mother reads. He said, "A newspaper about the livestock industry. She wanted to have a ranch and raise cattle."

▶ I recommended that he should go a cattle ranch, choose a cow, look deeply into her eyes, and release his anger by insulting her loudly while throwing a dozen raw eggs at her head. Then the consultant should mail a dozen raw eggs (placed in a beautiful box and well protected by cotton balls) to his mother.

48. A Korean woman feels that her life stagnated five years ago when she separated from her husband. She is a stylist in the fashion industry, and she wants to know what she has to do in order to evolve.

▶ I recommended that she create double models: for heterosexual, homosexual, and lesbian couples and also for a woman and her dog, a mother and her child, a grandfather and his grandson, two friends, and so forth. She should go from making ready-to-wear costumes to making specialty costumes (not equal but complementary).

49. A woman complains that her father despises women. For years he has repeated, "I cannot stomach these ignorant females." She is tired of wanting to prove to her father that she is intelligent. She wants an act to get free from him so she can do what she wants to do.

▶ I recommended, on the first day of her period, that she invite her father to dinner. At the end of the dinner, she makes him drink four drops of menstrual blood dissolved in a glass of cognac. The second day of her period, she writes what she wants to do on a piece of paper and wraps it around a tampon, which she inserts into her vagina. At the end of a few hours, she buries the paper in a pot, over which she will plant a flowering plant. The third day of her period, she sends this potted plant to her father as a gift.

50. A man has warts on his anus and emotional problems with his lover who cheated on him. He doesn't want to separate from him, but he feels like he cannot forgive him. We see that his father, now dead, never knew of his homosexuality.

- I recommended that he should go to the cemetery and rub his anus, smeared with honey, over his father's tomb saying, "Father, I am homosexual. Bless me." Then he must buy from a butcher the sex of a bull with the testicles, put them in a plastic bag, and tie this to his lover's genitals. With a kitchen knife, screaming out his pain, jealous with rage, he cuts the bag's cord. He throws the bull's genitals on the floor and rips them to shreds. Then he and his lover kiss and hug, gather the pieces, and bury them, sealing the "tomb" with a beautiful and very heavy rock.

51. A man wants an act that will help him open his heart. He feels unable to love, but he doesn't want to delve into the psychological reasons causing this pessimism.

- I recommended that he should dress up as a Buddhist monk and paint his face blue. He paints the right hand gold, the left hand silver. He goes out this way to walk down a very busy street, both hands supported on his chest as he recites, "I want to love, I can love, I should love and accept the changes love produces in me." He smiles at all the women who pass.

52. A young Jewish woman wishes to be independent from her family, but she feels guilty.

▶ I recommended that she should put three $100 bills inside a Hebrew Bible along with a photograph of her family. She then goes to the synagogue and leaves the Bible there, whispering, "I am paying for everything you have given me. I leave this here and freely follow my path."

53. A woman of forty wants to know why the company she created doesn't work. She has an emotional problem: she feels that her late husband wants her to fail because he is unhappy. She feels like his prisoner.

▶ I recommended that she should go to the cemetery where her husband is buried, carrying a photograph of him that she glues to his gravestone with her saliva. She says, "I understand why you are disgusted with me: you don't like that I buried you here. I will take you where you want to rest." She takes the photograph and carries it to the deceased's city of birth. She goes to the cemetery in that city and looks for a grave of someone who shares the same first name or initials as her husband, and there she glues with honey the photograph to this person's gravestone. She will feel free.

54. A young, attractive homosexual complains that he can't find lovers. He has lost his left hand, which has given him a complex.

▶ I recommended that he should stop hiding his artificial hand, which is an ugly imitation, and that he should paint it silver and wear a fancy ring on every finger. The ring for the middle finger should include a red stone.

55. A woman feels imprisoned in a psychic fortress. She doesn't trust any man because four people from her school raped her when she was seventeen.

▶ I recommended that she should carry out an act with four male therapists. She should dress up the way she was dressed when she was raped. The four men attack her, trying to knock her down. She defends herself. When she is about to be overtaken, with enormous authority, she throws out an order, as if she were speaking to dogs, "Fall down!" They fall down and remain there, quietly. She walks around them, caressing their bosoms, and tells them, "Now, come! I want you!" They get up and tenderly approach her. She puts a piece of sausage in each of their mouths. Looking into their eyes, she places in their hands the previously agreed-upon amount of money for their professional intervention and tells them, "Thank you for everything." Later, she buries the costume she wore for the act and plants a creeper over it.

56. A man who never had financial problems, due to belonging to a wealthy family, feels that he is not anchored in reality. He sees himself as too visionary and is afraid of going crazy. He lives in Paris.

▶ I recommended that he should go to a building with no fewer than five floors and that he should tell the doorman that the department of architecture at a university sent him over to measure the stairs with absolute exactness because he must clean them. He will give the doorman a tip for allowing him to do this. On his knees with a feather duster, he will clean the steps of all five floors. Then he will repeat this in another six buildings: one per week.

57. A man has emotional problems: he is very aggressive and domineering with his wife. He feels guilty. When he was a child, his mother was excessively severe.

▶ I recommended that he should put honey on his wife's feet and lick it off entirely. He should repeat this action for seven consecutive nights.

58. A woman, a poet, says she is unable to know her soul. She suffers because her parents (theater artists) wanted a boy, not a girl.

▶ I recommended that she should go visit her parents dressed as a man. She tells them to sit in front of her because she wants to carry out a metamorphosis in front of them. Following some musical rhythm, she performs a striptease, as slowly as possible. Once she is naked, she opens the lips of her sex and takes from her vagina a small quartz crystal rock. She then tells them, "Look at my soul, finally!" She puts the little rock in her mouth and swallows it. She makes them help her dress herself up as a woman.

59. A woman lives in anguish over the suicide of her father. Her mother, a woman with schizophrenic tendencies and the personality of an ogre, made her father's life unbearable; he couldn't take any more abuse from her. He took the car, left the house, and was found in the river. He had taken pills to kill himself. The consultant feels guilty for not intervening and letting her mother morally destroy him.

▶ I recommended that she put caramel candies in a jar with a skull label on it. She goes by car to the river of her father's suicide. She swallows all of the "pills." Then she puts her index finger down her throat until she vomits. From the vomit, she takes out the "pills" and puts them in a beautiful little bag. Then she gives them to her mother, knowing that she will devour them because she loves caramel candies!

A month after this act, I received a card that said, "When I saw my mother eat the 'pills' that I had vomited up, I started shivering, and then I felt the feeling of total liberation. Finally, I had found the spiritual peace I lacked."

60. A man who has a slight stutter experiences pain in his jaw muscle, the masseter. When he was a child, his younger brother suffered from mastoiditis and needed all of his parents' attention. He reproduces this pain, unconsciously, to attract attention.

► I recommended that he, in the morning for six days, glue to the side of the jaw in pain a one- by two-inch label on which his brother's name is written. He will keep this label on at all times, doing all of his laborious activities. If someone asks why he is wearing the label, he will respond without further explanation, "Because I have a problem." During the night, he will remove the label and bury it in a pot to which he will have glued a picture of his parents. At the end of the week, he will plant lavender in this pot.

61. A man says he has continuous bad luck: all of the businesses he starts fail. He was adopted as a child. His father convinced him to go into the navy when he turned seventeen. His bad luck started when he resigned. His now dead father wanted to be a sailor with all the homosexual imagery that implies.

► I recommended that he should buy a model warship similar to those on which he served. Once armed with the ship, he should go to visit his father's grave site dressed in uniform as an official sailor. Once there, he removes his uniform and places it on the gravestone along with the boat and a plastic phallus. He says, "Enough! Quit cursing me! So that you can fulfill your dreams, I am giving you my uniform, a boat, and a phallus. Now, allow me to fulfill my dreams."

62. A filmmaker (of only short films) can't manage to make a feature film. This block has lasted for twenty-five years. This has happened to him because of his complex about having a small penis.

▶ I recommended that he should get in touch with a special effects artist and hire this person to make a plastic penis about twenty inches long into which the consultant can insert his own member. He should wear this artificial penis supported by the length of his right leg when he goes to a meeting with any producer. This will give him the confidence in himself that he needs in order to convince them to produce a feature film.

63. A man on whose genealogy tree there are many people who committed suicide, among them his father, wants to have a loving relationship with his family (with the seven people left) in order to free himself from depression.

▶ I recommended that he should go to see these seven living relatives carrying a water gun. He shoots a jet of water in each of their faces and laughs while doing so like a bad boy.

64. A woman, raised in a fanatical Catholic family who inculcated her with the idea that sex belongs in marriage and never for pleasure, cannot achieve orgasm with her lover. She always speaks in a very quiet voice, repressing her desires to insult or maybe to kill.

▶ I recommended that she should make love with her lover at midnight and scream for five minutes like a savage beast imitating a cosmic orgasm, so intense that she wakes up all the neighbors. At the same time she should tear a Bible apart. Having done this, the woman should pick up all the torn pages and make a ball with them, gluing them together with honey, and then send it to her maternal grandmother.

65. A man loses more money than he earns anytime he invests in any project. His father was a laborer and a Sicilian immigrant. I asked him how much he was willing to invest to cure himself. He responded, "$500."

- I recommended that he should buy a Sicilian hat and wear it for six days with a $500 bill underneath it, over his hair. Then he should go see his father and give him the hat as a present, leaving the money in it and saying, "These things belong to you." In this way, the consultant will return his father's concept of money and free himself.

66. For three years, a woman's gums bleed. She recalls that her mother had a similar problem. We see that, thanks to this illness, the consultant, whose father did not love her, identifies with her mother and, in this way, expresses her unfulfilled, incestuous childhood wishes toward her father.

- I recommended she carry a photograph of her mother in her bra, go see her father, and say, "Hug and kiss me on the mouth!" He, who has always rejected her, will refuse to do so. So she takes out the photograph of her mother, rubs it on her bleeding gums, and throws it in her father's face, telling him, "This illness belongs to you! I'm giving it back!"

67. A woman, whose father committed suicide by shooting himself in the throat when she was eleven, always pairs up with men who quit loving her suddenly and then leave her.

- I recommended that she go to her father's grave site with a pistol equipped with a silencer and shoot a bullet into his tombstone. Then she says, "Take this. I extract this bullet from my life to give it back to you." She leaves the pistol and a jar of honey at his grave.

68. A young man, a guitarist, feels like he is going to lose his creativity and is afraid of losing the love of his mother (a guitarist, too, but unsuccessful). We see that he is condemned to failure through the guilt he feels for fulfilling what his mother could not do. She unconsciously prohibits success.

► I recommended he ask his mother to invite him to dinner. He arrives earlier than expected. While she cooks, he offers to clean her guitar. He closes himself in a room, takes off his underpants, and carefully rubs them against the maternal guitar. He puts the underwear in a bag, and later, without washing them, he uses them to rub against his own guitar wherever he plays a show. In this way, he will have robbed permission to succeed from his mother.

69. A woman, to give value to her feminine creativity, has fulfilled the psychomagic advice of taking a stroll with seven gold coins in her vagina. Having put them somewhere in the house, she has forgotten where and can't find them.

► I recommended she should call her father and convince him to help her look for the coins because he caused her lack of self-esteem.

70. A man, a musician, loves playing his cello, but his family, all in business, pays him no attention because he earns very little money. He would like them to quit laughing cruelly at him and understand him.

► I recommended that he should invite all of his relatives to dinner. He should buy a used cello. At the end of dinner, he announces, "Now dessert!" He brings out his cello, puts it on the table, and destroys it with a hammer. Then he puts pieces of the cello on each guest's plate and pours acacia honey over them, while saying: "This is what you all wanted. Now eat the pieces of my dream." Then the consultant takes out his own cello and gets on top of the table and plays the musical passage he likes most, allowing those who are leaving, offended, to leave. The consultant cuts off relations with them and only continues seeing those who remain.

71. An older woman is not happy in her marriage. She would like to divorce but something prevents her. She wants an act to help her find equilibrium. I ask her what is the place she would most like to visit. She answers, "Greenland!"

► I recommended she buy a ticket to Greenland. Without consulting her husband, she should go for fifteen days. Then return. During her absence, she should sleep with the first man who propositions her.

72. A white-skinned woman cannot stop scratching her face (sometimes until it bleeds). We see that her mother, married to a black-skinned man, was unfaithful with a white-skinned man.

► I recommended that she should paint her whole face black with makeup and go see her mother to tell her, "This is the way you always wanted to see me because you feel guilty about being unfaithful to your husband! Give me back my face!" She should take her mother to the bathroom and make her mother wash her face. This done, she will persuade her mother to kiss her all over her face.

73. A man lives with a woman who, suffering excesses of rage, won't stop violently insulting him. An equally angry woman brought up the consultant: a mother who endlessly insulted him.

► I recommended that he, for twenty-eight days, should write on adhesive labels all the insults they say. Then pack all these labels together to form a ball. He takes his wife by the throat, rubs the ball on her lips, and screams, "I love you!" Then he sends by mail this jumble of labels to his mother.

74. A man firmly believes that he was a victim of sexual abuse when he was a child. But he doesn't remember anything. He very often feels like vomiting. He represses a tremendous anger toward a man in his family. Which one?

▶ I recommended that he put on the floor in his bedroom a photo of each male relative. (He has two brothers, a father, three uncles, and a grandfather.) Next, as it is very likely that he was forced to swallow semen, the consultant should drink a gallon of milk and wait for the sensation to vomit to arrive. His body, independent of his mind, will choose the predator's photo through the vomit.

75. A woman wants to reconcile with her father who, before dying, sent her a letter full of insults and reproaches.

▶ I recommended that she should go to the cemetery and give her father's tomb ferocious lashes, burn the letter there, and, finally, paint on the tomb with a brush soaked in honey the word *love*.

76. A woman who is an actress and tourist guide feels that everything seems difficult. She wants to find the pleasure to be alive. She feels that her mother never gave her anything.

▶ I recommended that she should buy eight quail eggs and hard-boil them, then write on their shells the word *mother* and swallow them one at a time without chewing them. She then should drink two liters of milk and vomit in a toilet. She buries the vomit in a pot where, afterward, she plants a hydrangea. Then she sends a letter to her mother saying, "Thank you for having given me life."

77. A woman thinks her parents didn't want her to be born. They never gave her the means to develop herself. She complains, "They have killed my life! No one sees me. Everyone despises me."

▶ I recommended that she should hire a marble mason to make

a marble headstone with her name and birthdate on it, a dash, and then her birthdate again (for example, 1985–1985) to symbolize that she died when she was born. Then, for seven days, she takes a walk on the street with the headstone attached to her back in such a way that all the curious people can read the inscription. Afterward, with a hammer, she reduces the marble to dust, gathers the dust, puts it in an urn, and then scatters it in the sea.

78. A woman suffers because her parents criticize her sexual life. Every time they feel her enthusiastic about a man, they treat her like they would a prostitute. So each time she sees them, she adopts a childish attitude. What can she do to assert herself in their presence?

► I recommended that she should invite them to dinner in a restaurant. She arrives late and with a friend dressed as a gorilla, whom she introduces to her parents as her boyfriend, and then tells them, "I already paid the bill. You will have to eat without me. I am leaving right now because I'm dying to fuck this monkey." Then she leaves, embraced by the big animal.

79. A married woman feels overwhelmingly dominated by her husband. She is convinced that men have more power than women. What does she have to do to feel superior to him?

► I recommended that she should give him a glass of very good quality wine into which she has poured a drop of her blood. She does this for ten days (each time, the drop of blood will be extracted from a different finger).

80. A woman has had heartburn ever since her mother told her that due to suffering from unbearable vomiting attacks while pregnant she wanted to abort her.

▶ I recommended that she should drink a liter of milk each night, and then vomit into a carafe through a funnel. She does this for nine nights in a row, then sends it to her mother, who is very superstitious and believes in the power of witches. This vessel, with the cork sealed with wax, is accompanied by a card that reads, "This carafe contains water blessed by a shaman. If you bury the contents in your garden, all the plants will grow with exuberance."

81. A woman has enormous difficulties earning money. In her family, the women have been undervalued. Her grandparents, who were very wealthy, in order to affirm their sons' virile power only gave them the right to earn money working: the women were to dedicate themselves to the home and receive a weekly allowance from their husbands.

▶ I recommended that she should go to the cemetery and glue with honey a $100 bill on the gravestones of each grandparent and say, "This is the money that you forced me to take! I am giving it back to you! Now I am going to earn my own working in what I want to!" Then she will leave without looking back.

82. A woman, mother of four, in spite of the fact that her husband provides generously for her, wants to leave everything and go to a deserted island to write a book. She knows it is a dream, but she wants to find the way to fulfill this dream.

▶ I recommended that she design a room in her home that is exclusively for her where no one else, not even her children or her husband or the assistant, can enter. There, she will have only a desk, a chair, and a thick notebook. Every day, at six in the morning, she will get up and shut herself in this room for an hour to write her book, seated with her feet placed in a basin full of sand.

83. A woman with no psychoanalysis culture feels confused. Her father died of a heart attack when she was twelve years old. She idealized him. No other man could take his place. Without knowing why, this love made her feel guilty.

▶ I recommended (in order to become aware of the repressed incest wish) she should go to the church to confess. During the confession, she tells the priest, "Father, I am here because I am in love with you, and I want you to make love to me. We will have a baby as beautiful as Jesus." Then she should lift her skirt and urinate in this space. I promised her that if she did this, she would no longer feel confused.

84. A woman has felt attracted to a man. They have seen one another many times without ever making love. This has lasted for five years. She thinks he, feeling insanely timid and being a romantic, will label her an "easy" and shameless woman and not see her again if she proposes to him that they sleep together. What to do?

▶ I recommended that she buy a small turquoise stone and go to him and say, "I have consulted a medium and was told that we were, in another life, a couple. So that we recover our memory, I should give you this pebble but only passing it from my mouth to yours." If he accepts, this kiss will actually bring the two closer. If he refuses, she should forget him.

85. A woman always pairs with men who abandon her shortly after the relationship starts. This recycles the relationship she had with her father who committed suicide at fifty when she just turned fifteen. Her mother occupied all of the space of the disappeared. Between them they have raised her two little brothers who are today ten and twelve. She realizes that, in order to be faithful to her father, she makes the excuse to seek men who will not jeopardize the relationship she has with her mother. How to be free of this?

▶ I recommended that she put, on the Internet, an ad saying a young woman of twenty-nine seeks to have only one fiery encounter with a depressed married man who has one daughter of fifteen and two small boys. When this fifty-year-old man appears (don't try to verify if this is true), she must call him Roberto (her father's name) and make love to him and whisper the whole time, "Good-bye, good-bye, good-bye."

86. A short, skinny man with scoliosis complains that his "elders" don't take care of him. His father is a librarian, and his mother works in a bookstore. He wants to be a great writer, but he fears that he won't be able to live up to the literary demands of his parents (both failed writers).

▶ I recommended that he should walk with a backpack full of books for thirty-one miles. Then he burns these books and, afterward, goes to visit his "elders" and puts a handful of ashes in his father's hand and another handful in his mother's hand, saying, "This is your dead books! I am going to birth a living one!"

87. A woman works in a circus as a clown. She doesn't manage to do it with happiness. In spite of making kids laugh, she feels sad. Something is missing. We see that she left her family when she was eighteen. Her father wanted her to be an attorney. She preferred the circus life. He quit speaking to her for a long time.

▶ I recommended that she should go to her father dressed as a clown to tell him, "Accept that I will never be an attorney. Because of your criticisms, I have not been able to do my work well. I am asking that you be so kind as to make a small sacrifice for me. I want you to come see my performance, dressed and made up as a clown, and you sit in a corner so that I can be sure that you support me with your love." If she manages to convince him of this, she will discover the ecstasy of acting.

88. A woman has osteoarthritis, which is considered abnormal because she is young. Her maternal grandmother had an immense need for affection because she had been abandoned in an orphanage. Complaining that no one loved her, she enslaved the consultant's mother, asking continuously for massages in the parts of the body where the bones had atrophied. She grew up thinking that her grandmother received care and attention from her mother thanks to a sick skeleton. For this reason, in order to also attract maternal attention, she created osteoarthritis.

▶ I recommended that she should buy a human-sized, plastic skeleton and sleep with it for seven days. Then go to the cemetery and leave it there over the grandmother's grave saying, "I am returning your bones and your pain."

After fulfilling this act, her suffering disappeared; it briefly reappeared when she argued with her partner and felt abandoned.

89. A woman who sings very well cannot appear in public because she can't take the prying eyes. Her parents are not interested in what she does.

▶ I recommended that she sing through a beautiful ventriloquist doll that she designs. She should do that four times. The fifth time, she does it without the doll but dressed like the doll. Then she goes to visit her parents and persuades them to sit together and let her tie them up. She sings to them, undressing little by little, until she is nude. She takes the doll from the suitcase, sings through it a few measures, and then makes it talk, "I am a doll that your daughter had to employ in order to sing in public because you two do not show any interest in her art and she, therefore, feels invisible." The consultant tears the doll apart, gets dressed, and unties her parents. If they are not moved by this act, the consultant should not see them again.

90. A woman and a man who live together and smoked marijuana for ten years no longer feel stable now that they have quit. They feel that they lack roots in reality.

▶ I recommended that they buy, on credit, around-the-world airplane tickets. In each city they visit, they should hammer a thick nail into a street.

91. A woman who works as a secretary wants to change careers. She would like to make jewelry and lamps, but she doesn't dare do it because her parents always told her she had very bad artistic taste.

▶ I recommended that she make a brooch, trying to make it as ugly as possible, and an equally horrible lamp. She should give the brooch to her mother and the lamp to her father. She should tell them, "Admire the object I can make!" With this act the consultant will lose the desire for their approval. She will feel free to do what she wants.

92. A man has social complexes. He has desires to fulfill himself artistically as a sculptor but he doesn't feel he has the right to do so. He belongs to a family of bricklayers: his grandfather and his father and him, as well.

▶ I recommended he put twenty bricks in a pile and then destroy them by shooting them with a pistol. Then bury the pieces of brick together with an eagle made of plaster that he has sculpted.

93. A woman lives in constant anger because her mother ruled the house, and her father was not virile enough to put her in her place. Both are now dead.

▶ I recommended that she should go to a toyshop with a large childhood photo of herself on her chest. She should buy the largest doll she can find. She goes to the cemetery and leaves this photo on her father's grave, gluing it with honey and saying, "This is how I was when I needed a father. You were the only child, and I loved you as if you were my little brother." Then she will go to her mother's grave and strike the tombstone furiously with the doll. When the consultant has released all of her rage, she will say, "You too were a little girl. You were a tyrant in order to hide your weakness. I adopt you as a daughter." Then she buries the doll and plants a palm tree over it.

94. An actress says she is heterosexual but feels a powerful masculine force within her. We see that her father had homosexual tendencies. She, due to her childhood incest urges, is manly so he will like her. Now an adult, she has always rejected forming a partnership, in spite of innumerable adventures. What to do in order to decide to start a family?

▶ I recommended she create a one-woman show dressed as a pregnant man. She should explain to the public what it feels like for a man to gestate a child. This way she unites the childhood urges with the desire to love and to be a mother. She invites her father to the premiere.

95. A Parisian woman, whose Catholic grandparents raised her and instilled in her that sexual pleasure is a sin, feels that living in her body is forbidden and she only lives as a refugee in her head.

▶ I recommended that she hire a carpenter to make a cangue for her.

With this Chinese instrument of torture, she imprisons the neck and wrists, separating the head and the hands from the body, and goes to Notre Dame with a male friend who knows what the consultant likes. In front of the statue of the Virgin, the friend removes the cangue, and the consultant leaves it there at the saint's feet. She then asks her friend to go with her to a hotel room close by that will have previously been reserved. Once there, he blindfolds the consultant and proposes to make love to her.

96. A woman has suffered all of her life watching her parents argue and insult one another or she has endured days passed in their purposeful silence.

▶ I recommended that she go visit her parents and tell them that she suffers because she saw them separated all of her life. This separation prevented her from starting a family. If they want to be grandparents one day then they will have to face one another and put their feet together. The consultant circles them several times with a cord, tying them up. While she does this, she expresses all the anxiety she felt as a young girl. Finally, she tells them, "Like this, I love you! United forever!" She leaves, but she leaves them tied together.

97. A man says he feels his family like a heavy rock on his shoulders. His older sister died of breast cancer; his father, who never speaks, lost an eye; his mother suffers from epilepsy; and there has been sexual abuse. I discovered that the paternal grandfather, a farmer, caused all of this. He forced everyone to carry his or her own weight in order to cost him less, so he could spend as little as possible on the members of his family.

▶ I recommended that he buy a pair of boots, defecate in them, and then throw them on his grandfather's grave, exclaiming, "From this moment on, I am free of you!"

98. A woman with a limp lives possessed by an overwhelming sadness. She got polio when she was eighteen months old. Her parents didn't have her vaccinated; they never bothered with her. They belonged to families that, due to every kind of problem, did not know the happiness of life.

▶ I recommended that she look for a dried-out tree and nail into it pictures of all of her relatives along with a picture of herself as a child with her crutches. She then sets this tree ablaze and gathers up the ashes and dissolves them in a liter of blessed water. With this paste, she covers her whole body and sleeps like this. The morning after, she washes it off. Her sadness will have dissolved.

99. A woman is very annoyed because, for three years, her neighbor—one floor below her—makes unbearable noises during the night. I ask her what important event happened there years ago. She responded, "My mother died, a domineering woman and one of very bad character." We see that the neighbor below, a psychiatrist, represents the archetype of this invasive mother, a loved and hated mother who the consultant doesn't want to let go.

▶ I recommended that each time she hears an annoying noise, she should find the central place in the floor from which the noise emerges and place there a photograph of her mother. The next morning, the consultant should slide this photograph, with a black ribbon attached to it, under the neighbor's door. She repeats this action with photocopies until the neighbor comes up to ask what's going on. Being a psychiatrist, she will understand the problem and stop being noisy.

100. A woman, who in a few days will be thirty-six, complains that her life has not been easy; she doesn't have a partner, or work, or family, or material goods. She wants an act that gives her strength to begin a new cycle.

▶ I recommended that on her birthday she buy thirty-six nails, the biggest she can find. Carrying a hammer, she is to go to a place with hard earth and hammer the thirty-six nails there in such a way to make a star with five points. Afterward, she defecates on top while eating a red apple.

101. I received this card from Buenos Aires, Argentina:

> I am a worker employed by a travel agency and now very depressed from illness. They have removed three carcinomas from my left breast. I believe that one of the main motives is the internal conflict with my mother: a cold, distant, unloving, egotistical, frivolous, childish woman. What can you advise me?

I responded:

▶ You say your mother is cold, distant, unloving, egotistical, frivolous, childish. You should ask why? You will find the awful problem she had with her own father. He probably wanted her to be a boy, which causes the female offspring to act like a failed man. The breasts are called "mamman." If we remove an "n" we turn the word into "mama." These carcinomas are not yours; they are your mother's. Denounce your hate and let her breast-feed. You have to paint a bocce ball black, carry it in a bag next to the left breast, removing it only to bathe or to sleep. At the end of this time, send this heavy ball of steel to your mother with a card that says, "I return this to you; it's yours." Then you should find a woman who is nursing and ask her to let you nurse once per day for a week. Nurse with a pillow on your stomach, disguising yourself as a pregnant woman.

102. I received this card from Santiago, Chile:

At the beginning of this year, I fell into a depression that submerged me in terrible anxiety. . . . I feel that I can't go on. My body is heavy; I go around sad most of the time; I change my mind all day long; I am very sensitive; I perceive the negative things that people think. The two things that keep me going in life are writing or being with my boyfriend.

I responded:

▶ To get out of this depression, for seven Fridays in a row, go into your bathroom and take off all of your clothes and, starting with the feet, let your boyfriend cover your whole body (including the head and hair) in acacia or chestnut honey. When totally covered, he should caress your entire body—breasts, sex, even the anus, and also the soles of the feet—and then lick the breasts but leave part of the honey on the breast in the shape of a heart. He will pass the mirror over you so you can see the heart. Then wash yourself with warm water. Once cleaned and dried, get dressed in new clothes (shoes, dress, pantyhose, underwear) and go with him to a café to drink tea and have dessert. Don't wear the new clothes the next day: save them for the next Friday. At the end of this series of seven Fridays, tell your friends and relatives to call you by another name: a name that you alone should come up with without any help from anyone. After this, wear the new clothes whenever you want to.

103. I received this card from Guadalajara, Mexico:

I consulted with you because my eldest daughter of twenty was going through a very harsh crisis: she was always depressed, she inflicted self-mutilation, she didn't want to speak with me, or, if she did, it was very aggressive. She also had ferocious jealousy against her younger sister and there was always screaming in the house. You advised me to stage the death of my younger daughter. I lay her down in the middle of the room, dressed in white with a white sheet, surrounded by white candles and flowers. I dressed in black and called my older daughter (who was made aware that we were going to make an act but without knowing the details). Seeing the scene, she was enraged. As you told me to do, I said, "Your sister is dead. Is this how you want to see her?" She angrily responded, "Of course not! What do you take me for?" Next, I had to say, "So then revive her." Crying, she got close to her sister and said, "I want you to live!" Then, taking her hand, she continued repeating, "Live, please!" Her sister woke up and they hugged, crying. You told me that if she accepted to revive her sister, I should invite them both to dinner at a restaurant. This is what we did. We got ready and the three of us went out. Interestingly, the server who waited on us gave my eldest daughter a rose and said he thought she was very beautiful. When we finished eating, I suggested we go back to the house. To my surprise, my eldest daughter invited the younger one to continue the party, and they went out for the first time together and stayed out until dawn.

The following day, we went to bury the candles and to plant a plant above them. Several days have passed and I see my daughter smiling and animated; the relationship with me got radically better.

104. I received this card from Bilbao, Spain:

I am a twenty-three-year old man who asked for a psychomagic act during Christmas, 2005. The petition was to free me from a continuous and painful knot in my throat. When I presented the problem, you asked me, "Do you have sisters?" I said, "Three, older." You intuited that they could have raised me with the idea that boys don't cry. You advised me to dress as a woman with my sisters' clothes that best fit me and, dressed like that, stand in front of my father and cry. . . . My mother has always criticized men who dress as women, and me, perfectly programmed, I never put on a woman's dress unless I was drunk or to flirt with a girl. . . . Then I found another fear: Am I gay? Will doing this make me realize I like men?

The third day of March of 2006, I put on my sister's clothes before dinner. Dressed in a skirt, I went to the dining room. When they saw me they were surprised and laughed. The first comment was, "How pretty you are!" I didn't feel like crying but rather an absolute transparency before my parents. I told them, "This is a psychomagic act (they had already heard of you) and now I must cry but I don't feel like it." What I did was talk; I told them that I have felt very alone since I was a child, that I didn't hold any grudge, and I told them I love them . . . a magical, freeing moment. The days that followed, I doubted everything. I thought because I didn't cry it had not worked. I even felt the pain in my throat had increased. I also intuited that this showed me somehow that if I didn't cry it was because I didn't want to cry. Perhaps my tears were not sadness but rage. To my amazement, everything matured within me. Today, I cry. Not every day like a Magdelena. . . . But if there is a moment in which I need to cry, I can. Initially, just a little, but more easily each time. The painful knot in the throat has disappeared.

105. I received this card from Paris, France:

I went to see you in February 2007 because of a professional problem. Being one of the best students in my theater school, I was surprised to fail in all of my auditions. Why couldn't I have success in order to launch my career? You, after reading my Tarot, immediately asked me questions about my father. I told you that he, now dead, had been a mediocre actor who made a living with small roles for a television series. Bitter, he hated the world. His golden dream was to play the role of the protagonist in *Le Misanthrope* by Molière, which (in my school) I played many times.

You suggested I go my father's grave and leave a bouquet of flowers and a copy of Molière on his tombstone. Afterward, on the way back, I put on a long, blonde wig and a crown of thorns and blessed everyone I met along my route. I needed two months to gather the courage to do this. The long wig was easy to find, but to get the crown of thorns I had to hire a specialized florist to make it. When I had it in my hands, I quit making up excuses to delay the moment. At nine in the morning, I took the metro to the cemetery where I had not been in six years, since my grandfather's burial. I had not gone to my father's funeral. The trip took an hour. After much searching, I finally found the grave site. As agreed, I left the bouquet of flowers and the book, and I said, "*The Misanthrope* is your dream, not mine. I am giving it back. I will always love you, but I am not you. I will stop hating the world. I will allow myself to succeed where you failed." I put the wig on, the crown of thorns, and I took leave. My heart started beating rapidly. The hardest part had begun. I would need, at least, fifteen minutes to get to the metro.

As you asked, I began to bless the people in the street. "Bless you, Madame," "Bless you, Sir." Contrary to what I imagined, the people did not react with aggression. Some seemed astonished, but many thanked me without making fun of me. A woman asked me who I was, and I told her I was the Savior and I laughed. Jubilation was mixed with the fear and excitation. Another woman, after I blessed her, whispered, "May the peace of the Father be with you." I must have blessed forty people. Upon entering the metro car, I repeated three times loudly, "I bless you all." I sat peacefully, sure of myself. No one bothered me. A beggar got up and promised me, "God will give me back one hundred times the money I will give you." He gave me all the money he carried in his pocket. When I came up out of the metro, taking off the disguise, my eyes were full of tears. Following your advice, I kept the crown and the wig in a package under my bed for a week, then I buried them and planted a laurel tree.

For the fifteen following days, I felt abnormally tired. A month later I got my first big television role. I am going to play François Mitterrand in his youth. I am excited and anxious, but happy!

106. I received this card from Buenos Aires, Argentina:

During my travels to France, I asked for a psychomagic act because I have vitiligo, a skin pigment illness (the same disease Michael Jackson had), which is cured with medication sold in Cuba. Even though I have already been twice to La Habana for treatment, it always happens that another spot appears, which worried me a lot. You asked me what was the problem with the illness. I answered that the spots can grow little by little, and new ones can appear. You asked, what was wrong with that? I said that if the illness succeeds, it could make me completely albino. You asked me what was wrong with that. I didn't know what to say.

The act you recommended consisted of going out onto the street dressed only in shorts and with my whole body painted white. I should walk around a long time and have a white chocolate ice-cream cone. And, at the end of my walk, I should take a photograph of myself nude and then hang it in the living room of my home. This should be done with a lover accompanying me. This was the real problem.

When you prescribed the act, I was passing through a dreadful drought in the love sphere. The following week, just back to Buenos Aires, where the warm climate made the act easier to achieve, I found myself with a telephone call from my impossible love: a girl whom I adored and to whom I had given my number many months before.

I bought the makeup and prepared to cover my whole body. I began with the penis, which has a white spot on it. I imagined, as I painted myself, that the spot would grow larger, and I would be totally invaded. The thing didn't seem strange to me. I am a cartoonist, and I spend all day coloring. I put my shorts on and went out with my friend. I did well pretending to be relaxed. I wanted to walk as rapidly as possible like when someone travels down a road and passes a garbage dump and so holds his or her breath until the bad odor passes. I wanted to avoid relating to the girl in order not to embarrass her, but she took my hand. I realized that she accepted me, and that it wasn't a problem for her if I looked like this. There things started to change. Not only did I relax, I understood the importance of having made the act together with her.

A drunk yelled a greeting to me, and I responded the same; some workers having lunch on the street celebrated my passing, and I celebrated their lunching. Then, for the climax, I went into the main pedestrian street in the middle of the city where cloaked in tourists who come and go making purchases, I walked on the side where a Norteño music band was playing. The guitarist yelled, "I, too, want to be white!" A curious man asked me if I was saying good-bye to being single. Many people pretended to be disinterested. Upon arriving at my home, my friend took the photo of me completely naked, which I had framed and hung in my living room. Then I took a bath to remove the makeup, and my friend assisted me. I watched as the paint vanished and my color returned. Now the spots don't look like albino tumors expanding but like little white islands dominated by a large mass of skin color that keep the spots corralled. The act was good for me. My friend and I established a relationship of deep romance, and I no longer fear the vitiligo.

107. I received a testimony signed by the well-known French singer and composer, Arthur H (born 1966), the son of another well-known singer and composer, Jacques Higelin (born 1940):

> My father was an artist full of fantasy, history, songs, well connected with the imaginary world of a child. However, tormented by the murky past, he felt incapable of assuming a relatively balanced family life. The centrifugal force of the violence coming from his depths increasingly pushed him toward the incessant encounters: a constant drain that might give him a sense of confinement. The deep love that united my parents made it so that the separation was long and painful. My mother had to progressively detach, tired of the excess of absence and return and the infinitely unfulfilled promises.
>
> It was in this era that I began to expect it, completely impregnated (to the extent of making these things my own) with my mother's anxiety. Sometimes, my father would arrive unexpected from a tour, which was a beautiful gift. Other times, he announced his appearance—giving a precise date and time—but he wouldn't show; or he came finally after excruciating delay. I went from excitement, pride, and worry, to resignation, then deception, and finally indifference, mixed with a deep anxiety, and I thought, "Maybe he is dead and no one knows." When he finally arrived, I was already deep in depression, was not capable of supporting the energy of my father, and although I was happy to see him, I felt empty, impotent to expressing my feelings. As an adult, this sadness, although it had fulfilled me artistically, did not stop invading me. I lived in a state of constant delay, wishing to exist before his eyes in order to truly exist. The was no difference between these feelings and those of my mother, always worried and disillusioned waiting for the appearance of her lunatic and indifferent lover, preparing herself unconsciously for a future abandonment.
>
> Alejandro recommended a psychomagic act: Freud was wrong. It

is not necessary to kill the father (what would a dead father serve?) but to absorb him, make him live within. Symbolically, only once, transform yourself into your father, and now that you are a musician, a man of the public, turn yourself into your father in front of your audience, in a performance. Having captivated the audience let it be overwhelmed by the delay; you will not again be a child suffering before an unattainable, insurmountable father. You dress up as your father, and singing some songs, tell your public, "I am Jacques Higelin!"

My first reaction was rejection as if I had no right to play with something sacred. But, little by little, this act appeared to liberate me. When the chosen day arrived, I followed Alejandro's instructions to a tee. Before the end of my concert, I asked my musicians to leave me alone on the stage. I took out a suitcase that had been hidden behind an amplifier, and I threw it over a piano. It made a really loud noise. Then, in the middle of a deep silence, I asked the public, "Is there someone hidden in this suitcase?" Then, with total sincerity, I told them about my relationship with my father, his absence, the waiting, and also the love. While I spoke, I undressed until I was nude before the gaze of a shocked audience. "Here I am nude before you all, just like the day I was born." Then I opened the suitcase and began to take out my father's clothes, which had been taken from his home. "This is my father's familiar clothing that my father used on stage: a worker's jumpsuit, a belt of nails, an embroidered velvet jacket, and old sandals." It was a very intimate portrait; everyone laughed, so did I. "Now for an act of psychomagic, I will turn myself into my father." I got dressed in the clothes, and I began to sing one of his most well-known songs. As to the reaction to such a strange situation, the audience was silently respectful. I was very consumed by the feeling that I had surpassed something that was prohibited. When I finished the song, I undressed and thanked my audience for having participated in my dream. I threw my father's suit and then my own show clothes to the audience, making them participants in the healing. Again nude, I called my musicians to play our final number. This time I was completely myself, feeling a deep inner happiness. My collaborators were also happy, feeling the energy of freedom that was all around us.

Today I don't expect anything from my father. I don't have the need to exist in his eyes in order to truly exist. I don't have the need for him to listen to me in order to be able to express myself. I feel like there is still in my gut some rage, but instead of repressing it and turning it on myself, I can let it flow, express it, and transform it to make it fertile and creative, bestowing a vital energy on me and impelling me toward the world and toward others. I have decided to forgive my parents, free myself, and free them from the negative charge of the past, choosing to not see in them more than what life gives and all of the love that can be transmitted to me.

APPENDIX

Advice for Future Psychomagicians

Since psychomagic is the product of intense theatrical and artistic experience, it is not possible for someone with no practice in art to exercise psychomagic. One will find in psychomagic elements similar to a happening or a performance, poetry, painting and sculpture, or the martial arts. Other great inspirations for this healing art are traditional magic, shamanism, and the techniques of the folk healers. Whoever decides to dedicate him- or herself professionally to sharing psychomagic advice should beforehand practice the Tarot (such as I teach in my book *The Way of Tarot*) and learn the history of theater, the plastic arts, magic, shamanism, and martial arts. Reading the great poets should develop one's sensibility. One should also know the theories of psychology, to deepen awareness of psychogenealogy, and, above all, one should leave aside any religious doctrine. Prepare oneself with the same passion that a Buddhist monk works to detach from his individuality formed by the family, society, and culture. In this way one can overcome one's own discrimination and proceed impersonally during the consultations. Psychomagic creativity is not innate nor is it possible to achieve it quickly; it requires many years of dedicated effort.

Preparation to be a psychomagician can be divided into three steps:

Own oneself in daily life
Develop one's level of consciousness
Build an objective moral life

In the first stage, the aspirant should:

- learn to focus one's attention on a single theme, a single point, a single action
- overcome one's laziness; always finish what one has begun
- set out to do the best one can do
- never allow, even in solitude, unworthy attitudes from one's spiritual level
- eliminate all vices, mania, repetitive gestures
- control one's facial expressions; don't grimace
- be alert at every moment
- develop one's generosity
- strive to listen to others; avoid creating problems
- adopt a manner of speaking at the intellectual level of whoever is listening
- consciously give thanks for every gift
- explore one's physical possibilities
- quit stating one's opinion; don't lie to others or to oneself
- don't please oneself with pain or fear
- help the next person without making them dependent
- don't imitate or desire to be imitated
- don't take up too much space; make as little noise as possible
- respond honestly to every question
- don't be impressed by strong personalities
- don't appropriate anything from anyone

- don't cheat; don't seduce; don't follow fashions
- only eat what's necessary; protect one's health
- don't speak of personal problems
- don't establish useless friendly relationships
- be punctual, clean, neat
- don't envy the objects and successes of others
- speak what is strictly necessary; don't be an exhibitionist
- don't gesticulate uselessly anymore
- don't think about the benefits that one's actions or work will produce
- never threaten
- don't accept work that disgusts; don't prostitute
- always keep one's promises; respect one's contracts
- be capable of forgetting oneself and putting oneself in the other's place
- don't eliminate but transform
- never visit someone without a gift
- don't change directions because of criticisms or praise
- forgive one's parents and those who did wrong
- let come to one's mind all thoughts, feeling, and wishes, as huge as they are, and let them pass without identifying with them
- help others help themselves
- never accept an unjust no or yes
- overcome one's dislikes and transform them into kindness
- overcome one's pride and transform it into dignity
- overcome one's anger and transform it into creativity
- overcome one's miserliness and transform it into love of beauty
- overcome one's envy and transform it into love of the values of others
- overcome one's hate and transform it into generosity
- overcome one's lack and transform it into a love of the universe
- confront one's nightmares and overcome them

- do not allow into one's dreams behaviors that one would not admit while awake

In the second stage, the aspirant should:

- recognize one's subjective judgments and don't apply them to others as if they were objective truths
- understand why one is alive and what one should do in order to cooperate with the projects of the universe
- don't be at the mercy of one's body (knowing that the sense impressions can be misleading)
- don't allow illness or habit to affect the spirit; what we call depression impedes development
- don't inhibit one's desires (dissatisfaction) or exacerbate them (obsession)
- don't identify with negative feelings, engrossing bonds with people, communities and places, attractions or repulsions, fears, anxieties, and accumulated anger that will turn into hate
- sweep the mind of internal dialogues, daydreams, suggestibility, the desire to attribute the values of others to oneself, the vulgar egoism and the toxic imagination for amusement in order to forget one is mortal
- quit accumulating voraciously created false impressions or creating false behaviors plagiarized from important personalities
- wake in one's spirit faith (trust and not mere belief), hope (right effort to achieve that which is and not a neurotic desire to achieve what one should be), and charity (love of humanity, that which was, that which is, and that which will come)
- respect others not for the narcissistic deviations of one's personality—reflected in advertising, comedies, diplomas, prizes, remodeled bodies, economic voracity, excessive decoration—but for one's inner development

- develop harmony among one's four centers: intellectual, emotional, sexual, physical
- don't take cover in only one or two centers in order to repress the others, establishing inner barriers where one's thoughts, emotions, desires, and needs live in time and inconsistent intensities
- know how to rest one's mind in silence, one's heart without discrimination, one's sex feeling satisfied, and one's body with gratitude for being alive
- eliminate habits and repetitions, following one's legitimate desires and not copying what others do or comparing oneself with others in a constant competition
- realize that it is impossible to absolutely know beings and focus on verifying whether the established relationship obeys our constructive projects
- stop acting in order to accumulate merits
- don't escape but voluntarily confront one's suffering
- be capable of not wasting mental, emotional, sexual, and physical energy thinking that what one obtains for oneself is what others desire for themselves also
- never convert, through childish bonds, lies into superstitions
- realize that more important than what happens is how one reacts to it
- understand that one's conscious will is only free when it is exercised in union with the will of the unconscious

In the third stage, the aspirant must be able to honestly say:

- What will come, will come, and I accept it.
- My actions will not be guided by fear of infernal punishment or by greed for heavenly rewards.
- I will be what I am and not what others want me to be.
- I will accept the laws proclaimed by the community, but my

mind and my heart will remain free to think and to love what it desires.

- What I am not, I never will be. What I am truthfully, I will always be.
- I will stop declaring that my fulfillment is in the future. It is now when I should fulfill myself and make my potential fruitful.
- If God is not here, God is nowhere. If I am not here, I am nowhere.
- I am not going to scorn the present for the mysterious future.
- If there is a beyond, I don't need to know it now.
- When whatever has to come comes, if anything, nothing will impede my knowing it. If it is nothing, I will also be nothing. Why should I thus agonize over it?
- I will part with foolish ideas formed by anxious beliefs from childhood. I am what I am, doing not what I was or what I will be. I will live deciding to think that if now I dominate my spirit, I will reach peace in the future. If I am conscious, I will be capable of living with happiness in whatever dimension.
- So, without worrying myself about this "beyond," I will enjoy expanding the limits of my consciousness, knowing everything there is to possibly know without holding myself back to protect intellectual, emotional, sexual, or material barriers.
- To be able to know and to love others, I will learn to know and to love myself.
- I will understand that the best thing that could have ever happened to me in this world was that I was born.
- I will understand that what I call "to die" is a necessary transformation.
- I will understand that what there is in the world does not define the essence of the world. A lot of garbage in a gold chalice does not alter its quality: the garbage only messes it up momentarily.

- There is violence, egoism, fanaticism in the chalice, but the world is not this: in spite of the abundance of negative acts, it is a basic paradise, a land that I should clean and use in a positive way, to take the garbage out of the chalice and in its place put a diamond.
- Existence is sacred. I am sacred.
- Everything I obtain, I share with others.

Index

About the Author

Alejandro Jodorowsky was born in Tocopilla, Chile, in 1929. During his career as tarologist, therapist, author, actor, theatrical director, and director of cult films (*El Topo, The Holy Mountain,* and *Santa Sangre*), he developed psychomagic and psychogenealogy, two new therapeutic techniques that have revolutionized psychotherapy in many countries. Psychogenealogy served as the background for his novel *Donde mejor canta un pájaro* (Where a Bird Sings Better), and psychomagic was used by Jodorowsky in the novel *El niño del jueves negro* (Black Thursday's Child). Both of these techniques are discussed and explored in his book *Psicomagia* (*Psychomagic*), in his autobiography *La danza de realidad* (*The Dance of Reality*), and in *Métagénéalogie: L'arbre généalogie comme art, thérapie et quète de Soi* (*Metagenealogy: Self-Discovery through Psychomagic and the Family Tree*), written with Marianne Costa. He has also written two books on the therapeutic application of the Tarot: *La vía del Tarot* (*The Way of Tarot*), written with Marianne Costa, and *Yo, el Tarot* (I, the Tarot).